BRIDGES *Not* BARRIERS

WHAT KEEPS PEOPLE FROM CHURCH
AND WHAT THE CHURCH CAN DO ABOUT IT

DERRICK KITAYIGA

Copyright 2025 by Derrick Kitayiga

All rights reserved, including the right to reproduce this book or portions thereof in any form whatsoever. For permission requests, write to the author at Kitayigaderrick9@icloud.com.

Interior and cover design by Inksnatcher.com.

Published by Faithfull Books.

Printed in the United States of America.

LCCN record available at https://lccn.loc.gov/Library of Congress Cataloging-in-Publication Data

Names: Kitayiga, Derrick, author

Title: Bridges Not Barriers: What Keeps People from Church and What the Church Can Do About It

Subjects: | BISAC: RELIGION / Christian Church / Growth | RELIGION / Christian Ministry / Evangelism | RELIGION / Christian Life / Social Issues

Description: First edition. | Faithfull Books, Sacramento, CA, 2025. | Summary: "A call for Christians to tear down the barriers that push people away and build churches where everyone can genuinely belong." —Provided by publisher.

Identifiers: LCCN 2025924387 | 979-8-9901108-2-3 (paperback) | 979-8-9901108-5-4 (e-book)

Unless otherwise noted, all Scripture quotations are from The Holy Bible, English Standard Version ® (ESV ®), copyright © 2001 by Crossway, a publishing ministry of Good News Publishers. Used by permission. All rights reserved.

For information about special discounts for bulk purchases, please contact the author at kitayigaderrick@icloud.com.

CONTENTS

Introduction v
How to Use This Book ix

PART I
WHAT KEEPS PEOPLE FROM CHURCH 1

1. The Barrier of Judgment 3
2. The Intellectual Barrier 21
3. The Cultural Barrier 35

PART II
THE WOUNDS THAT DRIVE THEM AWAY 51

4. The Failing Leaders Barrier 53
5. The Barrier of Exclusion 71
6. The Barrier of Filtered Faith 85

PART III
BUILDING BRIDGES THAT LAST 99

7. Beyond Sunday Performance 101
8. Creating True Welcome 121

Conclusion: From Ritual to Relationship 131
A Final Note 144
About the Author 145

INTRODUCTION

"Church just isn't for people like me."

A teammate I have always admired, one who has treated me with consistent kindness, looked me in the eye as he said it. His honesty forced me to question why my friends did not feel welcome in church when I felt I was with my spiritual family there. I wanted to share my life openly with my friends and share what mattered to me, but if they didn't want to come to church, I felt like something must be wrong and that perhaps I could do something about it. I wanted them to share my appreciation of church.

Growing up in my home city of Kampala, Uganda, I spent much of my life in my local neighborhoods and on soccer fields, making many friends along the way—most of them friends of other faiths or of no faith at all. One of the great things about such friendships is that I was able to have real spiritual conversations with most of them, to the point where they started calling me "Pastor." They were curious, often vulnerable, and wanted to know about Jesus. But inviting them to church seemed to cause them to put up an instant barrier.

I could no longer ignore the fact that church was thought of as an unpleasant place to be for nonbelievers. That teammate's statement showed me that Christians *must* listen to why people stay away and find solutions to draw them in.

These are the reasons Christians need to hear and understand, so they can see the barriers they subconsciously put up to people living outside their safe church "bubble." Not all my friends who have visited a church have had a negative experience, and some friends have gone but never encountered the gospel in its simplicity; others have experienced it, but told me the encounter left them feeling ashamed or controlled—outsiders' perceptions Christians must reckon with. I understood their hesitation to visit a church. As an immigrant, I was treated differently in some churches once I moved to the US. With every new story I heard, I started to feel the call to steer the church toward facing the kinds of questions in a way that opens church doors wide rather than shuts them tight.

This book is for believers who seek deeper empathy for their neighbors. It covers specific barriers outsiders face, examined in light of Scripture, to help Christians respond with love. I long for this.

I have split this book into three sections:

1. Understanding the Barriers
2. The Wounds That Drive People Away
3. Building Bridges That Last

Each section addresses two to three obstacles to drawing people to church and examines them in the light of Scripture and of compassion. I have included stories of individuals' spiritual uncertainty, emotional scars, cultural estrangement, and moral conflict. I have approached the task with the hope of helping Christians learn how to draw others in.

I am convinced the church can be so much more—more welcoming, more reflective, more patient, more like Christ. Jesus never stepped away from the wounded, the wondering, the marginalized, or the doubtful; He stepped *toward* them. He told sto-

INTRODUCTION

ries, asked questions, and led with mercy. Christians must reflect Him by moving toward those who feel unwelcome.

Each chapter will challenge Christians to reflect, ask hard questions, and confront complacency. I tackle sensitive topics—church hurt, sexuality, politics, rules, cliques, busyness, and power abuse—precisely because silence and judgment only widen the hurt. We must honestly ask ourselves if our words and actions build bridges or erect barriers between the church and seekers.

At the heart of this book is love—love that listens, love that cares, love that seeks to understand. Jesus made an absolute promise: "All that the Father gives me will come to me, and whoever comes to me I will never cast out" (John 6:37). Never. Not 'unless they're dressed wrong' or 'unless they can't tithe.' Never. So let's keep His promise.

HOW TO USE THIS BOOK

If you're holding this book, you probably fall into one of three categories:

1. **You're part of a church** and you're wondering why your friends, coworkers, or family members won't come with you on Sunday mornings. You love your church, but you're starting to see it through their eyes, and you're realizing there might be barriers you've never noticed before.

2. **You're a church leader**—a pastor, elder, small group coordinator, or volunteer—and you're tired of watching people slip out the door and never return. You want your church to be a place where everyone feels genuinely welcome, but you're not sure where to start or how to create lasting change.

3. **You're on the outside looking in.** Maybe you've been hurt by the church. Maybe you're curious about faith but intimidated by Christians. Maybe you grew up in church and walked away, or maybe you've never been and you're trying to figure out if there's anything there for you.

   Wherever you are, this book is for you.

1. If You're Reading as an Individual Believer

Start with Part I. These chapters will help you see the barriers your friends and neighbors face—barriers you might not even realize exist. As you read, think about specific people in your life. When I talk about judgment, picture your tattooed coworker. When I discuss intellectual barriers, think about your skeptical college roommate. When I describe cultural barriers, remember your Muslim neighbor.

Don't skip the "What Churches Can Do" sections just because you're not in leadership. These aren't just for pastors; they're also for anyone who wants to be part of the solution. You might not be able to change your church's entire culture overnight, but you can do the following:

1. Welcome the person sitting alone next Sunday.
2. Invite someone to coffee who seems lost.
3. Speak up when you hear judgment in a small group.
4. Ask better questions when someone shares their doubts.
5. Model the kind of welcome you wish your church offered.

Use the stories in this book to start conversations. Share them with your small group. Talk about them over dinner with Christian friends. Ask each other, "Are we building bridges or barriers?"

2. If You're Reading as a Church Leader

I wrote this book with you in mind, but I need to warn you that some of what I've written will be hard to read. I talk about leadership failures, about churches that wound people, about systems that exclude. If you find yourself getting defensive, I understand. But I'm asking you to push through that defensiveness and really listen to what the wounded, the excluded, and the seeking are saying.

Here's how I suggest you use this book:

Don't read it alone. Go through it with your leadership team, your elders, your staff. Read a chapter together and then discuss it honestly. Ask each other: "Is this happening in our church? Are we creating these barriers without realizing it?"

Listen for patterns. If multiple chapters resonate—if you're recognizing your church in the stories of judgment, exclusion, and superficial welcome—that's not condemnation, that's information. That's the Holy Spirit showing you where to start.

Prioritize implementation over information. Don't just read this book and put it on a shelf. At the end of each chapter, discuss the content with your team and identify one concrete action you can take in the next thirty days. Just one. Then do it. Then move to the next chapter.

Use the "What Churches Can Do" sections as starting points, not prescriptions. Your church is unique. Your community is unique. What works in a 2,000-person megachurch won't work the same way in a fifty-person rural congregation. Adapt these suggestions to your context. The principles are universal, but the practices should be personalized.

Be patient with pushback. When you start making changes—when you challenge assumptions about dress codes or politics or who gets to serve—some people will resist. That's normal. Don't let resistance stop you, but don't steamroll people either. Bring them along. Explain why you're making changes. Share the stories from this book that moved you. Help them see what you're seeing.

Consider a church-wide study. If your congregation is ready, work through this book together—in small groups, in Sunday school classes, in sermons. Create space for honest conversation about where you've failed and where you want to grow. The questions at the end of each chapter can guide these discussions.

3. If You're Reading as a Seeker

First, thank you for being willing to pick up a book about church when church might be the last place you want to be. Thank you for not giving up on the possibility that there's something real here, even if you've only encountered counterfeits so far.

You don't have to read this book cover to cover. Start with the chapters that resonate with your experience:

- Been judged for how you look? Start with Chapter 1.
- Struggling with intellectual questions? Go to Chapter 2.
- Feel like Christianity would mean abandoning your identity? Chapter 3 is for you.
- Been wounded by a pastor or church leader? Chapter 4 might be painful but healing.
- Feel excluded because of politics or other differences? Chapter 5.
- Think Christianity is just what you see online? Chapter 6.
- Feel like church people are fake or hypocritical? Read Chapter 7.

And here's what I want you to know: The ways you've been hurt, excluded, or dismissed aren't how Jesus treats people. I know that's easy to say and harder to believe when Christians have shown you otherwise. But as you read, I'm asking you to try to separate Jesus from His followers. We get it wrong a lot, but He never does.

The "What Churches Can Do" sections might frustrate you. You might think this is what they should have been doing all along. You're right. But maybe seeing what churches could be will give you hope that somewhere there's a community that actually lives this way. And if you can't find one, maybe you're the person who'll help create one.

A NOTE ON DISCUSSION QUESTIONS

At the end of each chapter, you'll find questions designed for group conversation or personal reflection. If you're reading alone, journal through them. If you're reading with others, don't rush past them. The questions are where the real work happens—where you move from reading about barriers to actually identifying and dismantling them.

MY PRAYER FOR YOU

Whoever you are, wherever you're starting from, I'm praying that this book doesn't just give you information but also moves you to action. I'm praying that churches become more welcoming, that believers become more like Jesus, and that seekers find communities where they can encounter God without having to navigate unnecessary barriers.

I'm praying that we stop losing people like my teammate who said, "Church just isn't for people like me."

Because it is. It absolutely is.

Let's build some bridges.

—*Derrick*

PART I

WHAT KEEPS PEOPLE FROM CHURCH

CHAPTER 1

THE BARRIER OF JUDGMENT

Growing up in a Catholic household, Sundays were steeped in tradition and ritual. As a child, walking into church felt like crossing into another realm. That building was a marvel—vaulted ceilings, stained glass windows, and echoing sounds all making God feel big and sacred. When the choir sang, their voices soaring and echoing through the sanctuary, I'd feel chills ripple through me. But beneath those moments of beauty was a quiet loneliness.

I'd sit in the front pew with the other kids, hyperaware of the adults' eyes behind me, their silent watching making me squirm. The rigid expectations—perfect posture, proper dress, impeccable behavior—felt like a checklist to complete, not a way to connect with faith. More often than not, I wished I could just stay home. While it pains me to think about the number of children who have not had the chance to grow up in this environment of reverence and awe, I can understand why someone might visit a church like this and never return. Those inflexible expectations can feel like a noose that gets tighter if you stay.

In some churches, I felt like an outsider, performing rituals I didn't understand. That experience taught me how easy it is for seekers to feel judged or unwelcome, and perhaps for something as simple as their hairstyle, clothes, or offerings.

Barna's *Spiritually Open* material (December 2022 survey) mentions that among those of no faith, 49 percent described Christianity as hypocritical and 48 percent described it as judgmental.[1] In Barna's "Doubt & Faith" write-up, the research states that people who are reluctant to affiliate with a church often say Christians seem "closed and judgmental" or "value being right … over helping others."[2] This fits with what my friends and I have experienced.

JUDGED ON HAIR

"Derrick, you and Andrew need to cut your hair. An Afro and dreadlocks? That's not how a good Christian should look." I was in shock. My Afro was an expression of my identity and individuality. Alongside me, Andrew tightened his jaw, but he did not say a word. Joseph did not stop there, however, and proceeded to quote various Bible verses, misinterpreting them to justify his remarks.

Those were the first words in my new church in Uganda that were really painful. I had considered the place to be my haven, but it felt like I was on trial. I loved my hair, and the way I wore it wasn't some test for my faith. I was not going to let my hair get in the way of my love of God, but I wasn't going to change it just because of an overzealous assistant pastor. I knew he had issues

---

[1] Barna Group, "Openness to Jesus Isn't the Problem—the Church Is," *Barna*, May 17, 2023, https://www.barna.com/research/openness-to-jesus.

[2] Barna Group, "Doubt & Faith: Top Reasons People Question Christianity," *Barna*, March 1, 2023, https://www.barna.com/research/doubt-faith.

with control, yet because of his persistent judgment, I eventually stopped going to that church altogether.

This is how churches lose members. It's also why some people never try out church in the first place.

JUDGED ON APPEARANCES

I'd invited my soccer friend to church, but he decided not to come because of the things he felt he would be judged for.

"Look at me, Derrick. Look at my tattoos, at these clothes." He pulled at his baggy pants, his full sleeve of tattoos on display as he did so.

I really wanted to assure him that he would be welcomed and accepted in the Ugandan church I was a member of, but the reality was that I understood his hesitation. I couldn't tell him he was wrong. In my culture and tribe, there were specific guidelines on how to dress for church. These customs, which I valued at the time, taught us about a man or woman's dressing etiquette. We were conditioned to think that tattoos were a form of rebellion or of the Devil, and that piercings were only for women. And men were to keep a shaved face, which was a tradition for a long time. It took me a while to accept that even a single church might have a different dress culture from another church, and that we cannot judge newcomers by it.

Having now been in a few churches, I find that Christians tend to judge people based on their appearances instead of embracing them, spreading the message that we are far more exclusive than welcoming. We are expected to bring people to God, but the barriers we set in place turn out to be inflexible. It upset me that I couldn't get him to come meet my church family because of how they might look at him, but there was nothing I could do about it. I couldn't make his fear worse by talking about how some churches talk about money.

JUDGED ON FINANCES

I'll never forget the day I learned that talking about money can get you in trouble in America.

As a fairly new immigrant to the US, I was still trying to figure out all the unspoken rules nobody tells you about. A gentleman from the church I joined had invited my friend and me out to his ranch to show us around. It was a beautiful property—wide open spaces, horses grazing in the pasture, stacks of hay lined up near the barn. I was genuinely curious about how everything worked, so as we walked past one of the massive hay bales, I asked, "How much does a stack like that cost?"

The moment the words left my mouth, I knew something had shifted. His whole demeanor changed. The friendly, open conversation we'd been having just stopped. He gave me a short answer and moved on quickly, but the warmth was gone. I felt it, even if I couldn't fully understand why. Later, my friend pulled me aside and explained, "You don't ask people about money here. It's considered rude." I was stunned. Where I'm from in Uganda, asking about the cost of hay wouldn't raise an eyebrow. It's just information. But here, I'd crossed some invisible line I didn't even know existed.

That experience stuck with me, especially when I started noticing how churches in the US talk about money. Or rather, how they don't and then suddenly do in ways that feel intense.

I remember one of the first churches I visited after moving here. The service was great—good music, solid preaching. But then came the offering. The pastor spent what felt like fifteen minutes talking about tithing, about the importance of supporting the church, about how God blesses those who give. There were envelopes in the pews with boxes to check for different giving levels. People were passing around plates, and I could feel eyes on me, wondering if I'd contribute. I didn't know what to do. I was a broke college student living off financial aid and part-time work. I wanted to give, but I also had rent due and barely enough for groceries. And more than that, I felt this pressure—like my worth in that room was being measured by whether I put something in the plate. I know that wasn't the intention. I know churches need money to operate, and I believe in supporting the work of God. But in that moment, as a newcomer trying to find my place, it felt less like worship and more like a test I wasn't ready to pass.

What made it harder was that I'd come from a church back home where giving was taught differently. My pastor there always said, "Give what you can, when you can, with a joyful heart. God doesn't need your money. He owns everything, but giving is a way we participate in His work." There was no pressure, no tracking, no emphasis on amounts. People gave because they wanted to, not because they felt they had to. Discussing financial topics such as giving and charity tended to be more liberating. Here, it felt different.

Some churches seem more focused on budgets than on building the kingdom. I don't want to sound judgmental, because I understand the reality. Churches have bills. Staff need salaries. Ministries need funding. I get it. But I also know what it feels like to walk into a place as a newcomer and immediately sense that your financial contribution is part of the equation for whether you belong.

The contrast became even clearer when I finally found a church that felt like home. They mentioned giving, sure, but it was brief, almost casual. "If you're a guest, please don't feel obligated to give. This is on us today. If you're part of our community and want to support what we're doing, there are ways to give listed in the bulletin." That was it. No pressure, no guilt, no long speeches. What they did instead was invest in relationships.

People invited me to lunch. They asked about my story, my struggles, my hopes. They made space for me to be part of things without requiring anything in return. And after a few months, I wanted to give. Not because anyone pressured me, but because I felt like I belonged, like this was my community, and I wanted to support what God was doing through them. That's when I realized that people don't give to institutions. They give to the communities they're part of. And you can't guilt or pressure someone into feeling like they belong. Belonging comes first. Giving follows.

I think about that hay bale conversation a lot. I think about how something that felt so natural to me—just asking a simple question—was received so differently than I expected. And I wonder how many people walk into our churches and experience the same kind of cultural disconnect when it comes to money. How many people hear the emphasis on tithing and think, *This isn't for me?* How many newcomers feel like they're being sized up based on what they can contribute?

I'm not saying churches should never talk about giving. I'm just saying maybe we need to be more aware of how it lands, especially for people who are new, who are struggling, who come from places where money is talked about differently or not at all. Because at the end of the day, the gospel isn't about the money we bring to the table. It's about what Jesus already did. And if we're not careful, our emphasis on giving can make it feel like the opposite—like acceptance is something we have to buy our way into.

That's not the church I want to be part of. And I don't think it's the church Jesus built.

JUDGED ON PAST ACTIONS

People can even go to a church for a few weeks or months, but when they share their pre-Jesus stories, people start to look at them differently—as if they are the sum of the mistakes they have made instead of brand-new believers. Most individuals join a church precisely because they have made the decision to change. Yet instead of being met with grace, they are often met with suspicion—measured by what they once were rather than who they are becoming.

Every believer has a past; that's the very reason grace exists. The church was never meant to be a museum of the perfect but a hospital for the broken. When people come seeking healing, they shouldn't have to prove they deserve it. Jesus didn't ask the woman at the well to fix her life before offering her living water. He met her in her story, and from that meeting came transformation.

When we judge someone by their history, we forget our own. Growth takes time, and sanctification is a process, not a prerequisite. The most powerful testimonies often come from those who once stumbled the hardest. If we can't make space for the messy middle—the in-between of redemption—we risk turning the church into a courtroom instead of a community of restoration.

Grace does what judgment never can: it gives people room to change. And when the church chooses grace first, lives begin to unfold into something new.

HOW CHURCHES JUDGE NEWCOMERS (OFTEN WITHOUT REALIZING IT)

The irony of church judgment is that most Christians don't think they're doing it. We genuinely believe we're welcoming. We smile at the door, we shake hands, we say "Glad you're here." But judgment doesn't always announce itself with pointed fingers and harsh words. Often, it's quieter than that. It's in the raised eyebrow, the awkward silence when someone mentions their living situation, the assumption that everyone can afford to tithe ten percent. It's in the unspoken codes, cultural expectations, and invisible rules that insiders know but newcomers have to stumble through.

When you're on the inside, you don't see these barriers. They're just "how we do things." But when you're on the outside trying to get in, every one of these unspoken rules feels like a test you might fail.

I've experienced this from both sides. I've been the newcomer walking into spaces where I immediately felt out of place, and I've been the insider who didn't realize I was contributing to an environment where others felt judged. Both positions have taught me that judgment in the church often comes from a place of comfort with our own norms rather than from intentional cruelty. We create cultures that work for us, and then we assume they should work for everyone.

But they don't.

Appearances: We make assumptions about people's spiritual maturity, their character, even their salvation based on how they look, and make snap judgments about who someone is and whether they "fit" in our church. Jesus never did this. He looked at hearts, not spaghetti straps. He welcomed tax collectors and prostitutes, people whose appearance and reputation would have made them unwelcome in any respectable religious gathering. But we've somehow convinced ourselves that there's a "Christian" way to look, and anyone who doesn't conform to that image is suspect. My soccer friend wasn't rejecting Jesus by turning down my invitation but instead protecting himself from the rejection he expected from Jesus's followers. And that's on us. We've created an environment where people have to present a certain image just to feel like they might be welcome.

Lifestyle: Someone mentions they're living with their boyfriend, and suddenly they're a project to be fixed rather than a person to be known. Someone shares that they're going through a divorce, and we start whispering about what they must have done wrong. Someone admits they struggle with addiction, and we're not sure if we want them around our kids. This kind of judgment is particularly insidious because we dress it up as "upholding biblical standards" or "not compromising on truth." But there's a difference between holding to biblical teaching and using that teaching as a weapon to keep certain people at arm's length. Transformation happens in the context of relationship, not as a prerequisite for it.

When we make people's behavior a barrier to belonging, we're essentially saying, "You can come to church once you've already figured out how to live like a Christian." But that's backward. Church is supposed to be the place where broken people find healing, where lost people find direction, where sinners—all of us—find grace.

Giving: When we emphasize giving in ways that make newcomers feel like their financial contribution is being evaluated, we've crossed a line. When giving feels transactional—when they sense that their worth is tied to what they put in the plate—it stops being worship and starts being a barrier. The gospel is free. Grace is free. Salvation is free. But if a newcomer walks into our church and immediately senses that their acceptance hinges on their financial contribution, we've made the gospel feel like something it's not.

Rules and Lingo: We assume everyone knows when to stand and when to sit. We assume everyone can follow along with the liturgy or knows what "fellowship" and "benediction" mean. We assume everyone has a Bible and knows how to find the book of Ephesians. We assume everyone understands the unspoken social rules—who you can approach and who you shouldn't, what's appropriate to share in a small group and what's not, and how long you're supposed to linger after the service. But for someone who didn't grow up in church, all of this is foreign. And when we don't make space for people to not know, when we don't explain things or offer help without being asked, we're communicating that this space is for people who already understand, not for people who are trying to learn. Like in my Catholic childhood, I learned how easy it is to feel like an outsider in a space that assumes you already know the rules.

Politics: Churches have aligned themselves—sometimes explicitly, sometimes implicitly—with certain political positions, and anyone who doesn't share those views feels like they don't belong. We've turned voting records and opinions on hot-button issues into tests of orthodoxy, and we've pushed out people who love Jesus but see these issues differently. This is particularly painful because it divides the body of Christ along lines Jesus never drew. He didn't come to build a political party. He came to seek and save the lost, to reconcile people to God and to each other. But we've let our political tribes become more important than our spiritual family, and newcomers can feel that division the moment they walk in the door.

All of these forms of judgment—whether based on appearance, behavior, finances, knowledge, or politics—send the same message: "There's a right way to be a Christian, and you're not doing it." They make the church feel like a club with membership requirements instead of a family with open arms. They make grace feel conditional. They make the gospel feel small.

Every time we judge a newcomer, we're not just hurting that individual. We're misrepresenting Jesus. Because Jesus didn't come for the people who had it all together. He came for the messy, the broken, the confused, the outsiders. He came for people exactly like the ones we're judging.

If our churches are going to be places where people encounter Jesus, we have to stop putting barriers between people and Him. We have to examine our own hearts and our own cultures and ask honestly if we are making it easier or harder for people to experience God's love and if we are welcoming people as they are or requiring them to change before we will accept them.

The answer to those questions will determine whether we're a church that grows the kingdom or one that keeps the door closed.

WHAT CHURCH MEMBERS CAN DO: CREATE CULTURES OF RADICAL WELCOME

But if we're serious about being the church Jesus envisioned, it's work we have to do, especially considering that "the latest religious landscape study (RLS), fielded over seven months in 2023–24, finds that 62% of U.S. adults identify as Christians. That is a decline of 9 percentage points since 2014 and a 16-point drop since 2007."

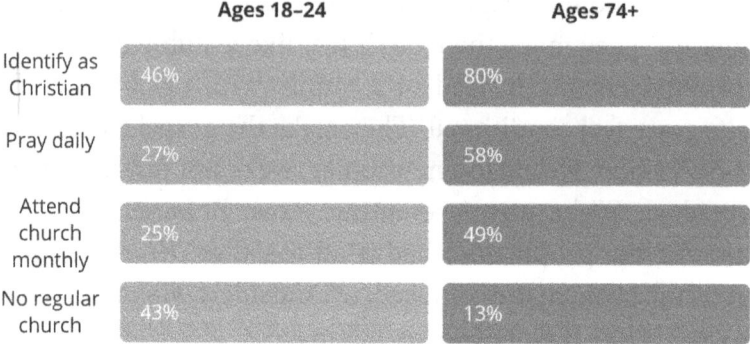

Figure 1. Share of U.S. adults who identify as Christian, Protestant, Catholic, religiously unaffiliated, and with non-Christian religions, 2007–2023/24. The long-term decline in the Christian share appears to have slowed or leveled off since approximately 2019–2021. Data from Pew Research Center's 2023–24 Religious Landscape Study.[3]

If judgment—in all its subtle forms—is the problem, then the solution is creating cultures of radical welcome. Not just being nice at the door, but fundamentally shifting how we think about who belongs and what we require of people.

I've been the person feeling judged, and I've also been the person who didn't realize I was creating that environment for someone else. Both experiences taught me something important: we're usually not trying to hurt people. We're just comfortable with what's familiar, and we assume everyone else will be too.

The good news? Once you see it, you can change it. Here's how:

---

[3] Gregory A. Smith et al., "Decline of Christianity in the U.S. Has Slowed, May Have Leveled Off," Pew Research Center, February 26, 2025, https://www.pewresearch.org/religion/2025/02/26/decline-of-christianity-in-the-us-has-slowed-may-have-leveled-off/.

THE BARRIER OF JUDGMENT

Notice who's being excluded, even unintentionally. Pay attention to who sits alone. Notice who leaves without talking to anyone. Observe which newcomers are greeted warmly and which ones are overlooked. You don't need to be in leadership to see these patterns; you just need to be awake to them.

When you notice someone on the periphery, do something about it. Sit with them. Ask their name. Invite them to lunch. These small acts aren't leadership initiatives; they're just basic kindness, and any member can do them.

Challenge your own assumptions. Ask yourself: Do I feel uncomfortable around people who look different from me? Do I make snap judgments about someone's faith based on their appearance? Do I assume certain people wouldn't belong in our church? These aren't accusations; they're honest questions we all need to ask ourselves.

I still remember the discomfort I felt walking into a young adults' group as the only Black person in the room. I almost didn't go back. Be the person who says more than hi to a visitor.

Speak up gently when you see judgment. If someone comments on a newcomer's appearance or lifestyle, you don't need to be confrontational. A simple, "I think they're great. I'm glad they're here," can redirect the conversation. If you hear gossip about someone's past, you can say, "That's their story to share if they want to. I'm just glad they're giving faith a try."

You have more power than you think. A single voice defending someone can make a difference.

Invite people in, not up. Don't just invite people to Sunday service. Invite them to lunch. Invite them to your home. Invite them into the messy, real parts of your life. That's where real welcome happens—not in polished settings but in genuine community.

Remember that you represent Jesus. This is the hardest truth I've had to accept: whether you like it or not, people judge Christianity based on how Christians treat them. You're not just a person with personal opinions—you're an ambassador. Your welcome or your coldness might be their first experience of the gospel.

I don't say that to shame you. I say it to empower you. You have the ability, right now, to change someone's mind about faith by simply treating them with dignity and kindness.

WHAT CHURCH LEADERS CAN DO: ESTABLISH SYSTEMS OF WELCOME

Speaking as both a member and as someone helping lead, I've learned that individual kindness matters, but it's not enough. A church needs systems. Your job as a leader is different from what church members do. Members welcome one person at a time. You create the conditions that make welcome easy, not heroic.

Start by actually listening to newcomers. Send out a survey to first-time visitors. Ask them specifically: Did you feel welcomed? Was there anything that made you uncomfortable? What would make you come back? Then listen to the answers, especially the hard ones. Don't defend. Don't explain. Just listen.

It might be that you can't see your own culture clearly anymore because you've been in it too long. Newcomers can see it in a way you can't. Their feedback is a gift.

Make explicit what's usually implicit institutionally. Create printed guides for newcomers. What happens during a service? What do the symbols mean? Where do I find things?

Make sure your website answers basic questions: Where do I park? Do I need to bring anything? What should I wear? Will someone talk to me if I don't know anyone? These aren't niceties. They're removing unnecessary obstacles to encountering God.

Develop a trained welcoming team, not just greeters. A greeter says hello. A welcomer makes sure you're not sitting alone. A welcomer remembers your name the second time you visit. A welcomer follows up during the week.

Train this team thoroughly. Teach them to notice the person standing alone. Help them ask genuine questions and listen to the answers. Make sure they understand that their job is to make sure no one feels invisible. Build a diverse team. The best welcomers aren't always the most extroverted people. Sometimes the quiet person notices the other quiet person sitting alone.

Create and enforce clear policies about money. This is where leadership really matters. You set the tone for how money is discussed in your church.

If you're emphasizing tithing in ways that feel pressured, stop. Teach about generosity as an overflow of gratitude, not as an obligation or a test of spiritual maturity. During the offering, make it explicitly clear that guests are not expected to give.

Consider whether you actually need giving thermometers, pledge campaigns, and multi-week sermon series on tithing. These might motivate your core givers, but they send a message to newcomers that their financial contribution determines whether they belong.

Be transparent about how money is used. When people see their contributions going toward meaningful ministry, they naturally want to give.

Design your space for accessibility. Think about a person with a wheelchair. Think about a parent with a young child. Think about a first-time visitor who doesn't know where anything is. Accessible parking. Clear signs. Handicap-accessible restrooms. A welcoming children's ministry area. These aren't extras—they're baseline hospitality.

Establish a follow-up system. When someone new visits, follow up within 48 hours with a text, a call, or an email: "We're glad you were here. We'd love to see you again."

If someone comes multiple times and then stops, reach out and ask what happened. You might discover they felt judged. You might learn something crucial about your church that you couldn't see from the inside. This is how you find out whether your welcome is actually working.

Have honest conversations about who leads in your church. Look at your leadership. Who has power? Who has a voice? Who's visible? If everyone looks the same, thinks the same, votes the same, you're reflecting your own tribe but not Ephesians 4. Look at who you're inviting into leadership roles. Are you inviting people from different backgrounds? Are you making space for people who think differently? Or are you only promoting people who are like you?

These conversations might be uncomfortable. They should be. They're also necessary.

Change what you measure. Stop measuring success primarily by attendance. Attendance matters, but it's not the most important metric. Measure how many newcomers are being integrated into the church community. Measure how many people feel genuinely welcomed. Measure spiritual transformation. Measure whether people are staying and growing. These questions are harder to answer than how many people came on Sunday.

I know this is a lot, but you don't have to do everything at once. Start with one thing. Maybe it's creating a follow-up system for newcomers. Maybe it's having an honest conversation about your leadership composition. Maybe it's rethinking how you talk about money.

But start somewhere. Because the systems you create either make welcome easy or make exclusion easy. Right now, what systems are you maintaining?

DISCUSSION QUESTIONS

1. Derrick was judged for his Afro, and his friend didn't come to church because of his tattoos. What are the unspoken dress codes or appearance expectations in your church? Are they biblical or cultural?

2. The author writes about the awkward silence when he asked about the cost of hay. What cultural assumptions do we make about money that might make newcomers uncomfortable?

3. Think about someone who joined your church and then shared their past. How did the community respond? Did it change how people treated them?

4. "When we judge someone by their history, we forget our own." Reflect on your own past. What grace did you need that you might not be extending to others?

5. The chapter lists several ways churches judge newcomers without realizing it. Which of these have you seen in your church: appearances, lifestyle, giving, insider knowledge, or political alignment?

6. What is one concrete action you could take this week to create a culture of radical welcome in your church or small group?

7. If someone walked into your church for the first time this Sunday, what would they need to know that nobody would tell them? How could you change that?

CHAPTER 2

THE INTELLECTUAL BARRIER

During my childhood, I found myself caught between discussions about God's existence in two very different classrooms—science and Christian religious education (CRE). In science, I learned about evolution and the idea that humans came from primates. In CRE, I was taught the creation story where God made humanity in His own image. Exposed to both at once, I struggled, even in those early years, to figure out which one was true. The conflict wasn't in my face; it was my daily reality.

My science teacher, with his sharp humor and quick wit, was incredibly persuasive. To keep my restless attention, he filled his lectures with jokes. One line I've never forgotten was his mock warning: "Don't be surprised when humanity goes back to being monkeys!" The funny way he said it was meant to make us laugh. Yet the power of science—facts, measurements, and the logic of experiments—stood behind everything he taught. Through that lens, he showed us the wonder of existence and, in doing so, deepened the conflict in my young mind.

He, with his experiments and graphs, made me feel that science offered real certainty, its results appearing as solid as the scientific instruments we passed between our desks. In stark contrast, my CRE teacher's stiff approach made every lesson feel like a formal inspection. I pretended to pay attention, folding my hands and nodding, though my mind drifted elsewhere. Science invited questions, offering the thrill of solving puzzles, while CRE felt like memorizing names of biblical figures, their ages, and the numbered laws that came in rigid order. Yet something stayed with me—the small, worn Bible I pulled out during quiet moments. Its words drew me back again and again. Rather than the lessons behind the stories, it was those pages and the characters' stories that held my attention, as if the book itself whispered of another reality I was free to explore.

I'm convinced that only by God's grace am I free from the contradictions that once threatened to trap me. As a young person, I was struck by the worldview of some of my peers who called themselves rationalists. Some even had a strange fascination with the idea of black magic. I found this confusing—how could someone believe in a rebellious supernatural power yet dismiss the Creator's power, the source of all life, as mere fiction? Scripture describes Satan as one who, once close to God, gave in to pride, tried to take God's place, and was thrown from heaven. The contradiction in their thinking left me shaking my head, and now I see it with the clarity that grace has given me.

As I grew older, the question of God's existence kept troubling me. I found myself caught between two worlds: the sciences, which explain the universe through data and observation, and religious belief, which affirms God without physical proof. The Bible simply states, "In the beginning, God created the heavens and the earth" (Genesis 1:1), yet modern science describes an initial singularity, the expansion of space and time, and the slow development of life across billions of years. How could these two stories exist together without contradicting each other? I was not alone. A 2019 Pew Research Center survey found that 73 percent of adults see science and religion as often in conflict, though only 30 percent say their own religious beliefs conflict with science.[4]

This tension has stayed with me, yet I'm not alone in wrestling with it. Some of my friends have wrestled with the same questions, especially during seasons of sickness and loss. When they don't have Christian friends to turn to, or when someone invites them, they often visit a church hoping to find answers.

FAITH AND SUFFERING

My close friend Caleb entered a season marked by crushing loss when his father died suddenly. The emptiness left by that death overwhelmed him. In the depth of his grief, Caleb turned his anger toward God. Why, he asked, would a loving God allow this to happen to a man whose greatest qualities were kindness and faith? The question felt impossible to answer. I've heard similar accusations in other voices—questions about God's silence and distance, each one making the struggle feel more real. Caleb's pain slowly pulled him away from church, though he kept trying to build some bridge between the faith he'd inherited and the brutal reality of what he was living through.

Caleb didn't arrive at easy answers following his father's death, nor did he find quick solutions to his grief. Yet as days turned to months, a quiet understanding settled within him: his crushing pain would not be in his future. As he grieved, Caleb encountered a deeper love, sensing God's comfort and peace in a way he hadn't known before. Over time, the distance between him and God grew smaller, and his heart changed. From

---

[4] Pew Research Center, "Perception of Conflict Between Science and Religion," *Pew Research Center*, October 22, 2015, https://www.pewresearch.org/science/2015/10/22/perception-of-conflict-between-science-and-religion/

the promise of the One raised from the grave, Caleb drew real hope—that the world's present brokenness and the weight of evil cannot be final. We, too, will be raised, entering a life beyond measure, where there will be no more grief and suffering.

The biblical character Job never got answers to his *why* questions either. We read thirty-seven chapters of Job demanding God explain Himself, and God's response wasn't an explanation; it was His presence. "Where were you when I laid the foundation of the earth?" (Job 38:4). Sometimes faith isn't about getting answers; it's about trusting the One who holds them. Caleb discovered that God's comfort wasn't in explanation but in proximity.

One thing Caleb also learned from going through his grief was that Christians are the hands and feet of God, and we are the tangible presence of help people can see as long as we are ready to give and minister. Thankfully, Christians stayed present in this case. I learned more about people's instant need for Jesus when evangelizing.

MEETING DOUBT WITH SOLUTIONS

James 2:14–17 asks, "What good is it, my brothers and sisters, if someone claims to have faith but has no deeds?" What's the point of telling a brother or sister who lacks warm clothing and food that everything will be fine, while doing nothing to actually help them? This hit me hard on the mission field. Christians are God's front line for relieving suffering. We're called to be Jesus with skin on—not just talking about His love, but showing it through action. When we feed the hungry, clothe the cold, sit with the grieving, and meet practical needs, we're making the invisible God visible. We're showing people that they don't need to doubt God because we are present to show His love. That's not separate from evangelism; it is evangelism. It's the gospel lived out in a way people can touch, taste, and experience. Without it, our words about God's love ring hollow.

Every time I went on a mission trip, I learned that we weren't just bringing the good news to people; we were meeting them as human beings with real feelings, and sharing their joys and their struggles. The heart of the gospel came alive in the camaraderie we built with people in unfamiliar places. Jesus didn't preach from a distance. He walked with people, shared meals, healed their wounds, and turned their deepest struggles into real conversations. We're called to this same kind of ministry, where people are never statistics, projects, or numbers to add to a report. They're treasured children of God who need His mercy, His love, and His grace made real through us.

People should never have to ask where God is if Christians are ready to act like Jesus. Doubt is normal, and wanting to understand God is as natural as breathing.

CREATING QUESTION-FRIENDLY ENVIRONMENTS WHERE DOUBT IS SAFE

The church has a problem with doubt and questions. We've created cultures where asking hard questions feels like betraying the faith, where doubt is treated as the opposite of belief rather than part of the journey toward deeper understanding. We've made intellectual curiosity seem dangerous, as if God is so fragile that honest questions might shatter everything we hold dear. And we're losing people because of it. Research by the Barna Group reveals that 36 percent of young adults who left Christianity cite "intellectual skepticism" as a major factor, and 29 percent say churches are out of step with the scientific world we live in.[5]

But that's not the God I've come to know. The God who created the universe with its complex laws of physics, who designed DNA and the human brain, who set planets in motion and established the principles that govern everything from gravity to genetics—that God isn't threatened by our questions. He's big enough to handle our doubts, our confusion, and our wrestling.

When I sat in those two classrooms as a child—science on one side, CRE on the other—I needed someone to tell me it was okay to ask how they fit together. I needed a space where I could voice my confusion without being shut down or made to feel like my questions were evidence of weak faith. Instead, I got a science teacher who made learning exciting and a CRE teacher who made faith feel like drudgery. Is it any wonder which one captured my imagination? In church, I felt like I had to choose between my intellect and my faith, between the questions that made sense to me and the answers I was being given.

The intellectual barrier keeps people from faith, not because Christianity can't stand up to scrutiny, but because we refuse to engage with the inquiry honestly. We give pat answers to complex questions. We tell people to "just have faith" or that "God works in mysterious ways" when they're wrestling with real tensions between what they observe in the world and what they're being taught in church. We act like doubt is a disease to be cured rather than a sign that someone is thinking deeply about what they believe.

Caleb's struggle after his father's death wasn't just emotional; it was also intellectual. How do you reconcile a loving God with

---

[5] Barna Group, "Six Reasons Young Christians Leave Church," *Barna*, September 27, 2011, https://www.barna.com/research/six-reasons-young-christians-leave-church.

senseless tragedy? That's not a simple question, and it doesn't have a simple answer. What Caleb needed wasn't someone to quote Romans 8:28 at him and call it a day. He needed someone who could sit with him in the tension, who could acknowledge that yes, this is hard; yes, this seems contradictory; and yes, it's okay to be angry and confused and full of questions.

The mission field taught me this lesson in a different way. When we went to unreached villages and people asked questions about Christianity, their questions weren't the neat, packaged ones we'd rehearsed answers for. They wanted to know why our God was better than their gods. They wanted to know how Jesus related to their ancestors. They wanted to know why, if God is good, their children were dying of preventable diseases. These weren't theoretical questions; they were life-and-death questions, and they deserved better than rehearsed talking points.

Creating a question-friendly environment means making space for the messy, uncomfortable, unresolved tensions that come with faith. It means admitting that some questions don't have neat answers this side of eternity. It means being okay with "I don't know" instead of pretending we have God all figured out. The tragedy is that we lose so many brilliant minds when we shut down questions from the doctors, the scientists, the engineers, the philosophers—people whose work requires them to ask hard questions and demand evidence. We tell them to check their brains at the door when they come to church, and then we're surprised when they don't come back. But it doesn't have to be this way.

Faith and reason aren't enemies; they're partners. God gave us minds capable of incredible thought, and He expects us to use them. Jesus didn't rebuke Thomas for doubting (John 20:24–29). When Thomas said, "Unless I see in his hands the mark of the nails, and place my finger into the mark of the nails, and place my hand into his side, I will never believe" (v. 25), Jesus didn't condemn him. A week later, Jesus appeared and said, "Put your finger here, and see my hands; and put out your hand, and place it in my side." He met doubt with invitation, not accusation. Then He added, "Have you believed because you have seen me? Blessed are those who have not seen and yet have believed" (v. 29)—making room for both the doubter who needs evidence and the believer who trusts without it.

God isn't afraid of our questions. Through the prophet Isaiah, He invited: "Come now, let us reason together… though your sins are like scarlet, they shall be as white as snow" (Isaiah 1:18). Even in a passage about sin and redemption, God opened with an invitation to reason, to wrestle, to work through the hard questions together.

A question-friendly church doesn't mean a church without conviction or truth. It means a church secure enough in truth to let it be tested. It means leaders are humble enough to say they don't know instead of making up answers to preserve their authority. It means creating spaces where people can bring their doubts without fear of judgment, where wrestling with God is seen as engagement, not abandonment.

When we silence questions, we don't protect faith; we shrink it. We make Christianity smaller than it is, more fragile than it needs to be. We push away the seekers, the thinkers, the people who can't accept things at face value. And we miss out on the deeper, richer faith that comes from wrestling through doubt to the other side.

WHAT CHURCH MEMBERS CAN DO: WELCOME QUESTIONS AND DOUBT

You don't need anyone's permission to wonder. If you're wrestling with whether science and faith fit together, if you're angry at God about suffering, or if you have doubts about core beliefs, that's not a character flaw. That's not evidence of weak faith. That's you thinking deeply about what matters most.

I spent years feeling like I had to hide my questions. I couldn't figure out why, and I couldn't ask. So I learned to keep my doubts quiet. I'm still recovering from that.

Stop waiting for permission to wonder. The questions you're afraid to ask are valid. All of them. Whether you're wondering how evolution fits with Genesis, or why God feels silent when you're suffering, or whether the Bible is historically reliable—these aren't threats to your faith. They're invitations to deeper faith.

Start by acknowledging your own doubts instead of burying them. Write them down. Talk about them with people you trust. Don't pretend you have it figured out when you don't.

Find people who won't panic when you voice doubts. Seek out friends and mentors who will listen without immediately trying to fix your thinking. Look for people who've wrestled with similar doubts and have come through with their faith intact. These relationships matter more than any sermon.

I'm talking about people who don't freak out when you say, "I'm not sure about this anymore." People who don't rush to defend doctrine. People who just listen and share their own struggles honestly. These people are rare, but they're worth finding.

Normalize doubt in your own life. When you're talking with friends about faith, include the real stuff. Don't just share your victories; also share your questions. Talk about the times your faith felt shaky. Share the doubts you're working through. When people see that you're wrestling and your faith is still intact, it gives them permission to do the same.

Participate in spaces where questions are welcome. When your church creates a Q&A session or a doubt-friendly small group, show up. Ask the things you've been wondering about. Bring your honest questions, not just your polished faith. When others see someone actually asking hard questions without being condemned, it changes everything. It gives permission to people who've been afraid to speak up.

WHAT CHURCH LEADERS CAN DO: BUILD CULTURES WHERE DOUBT IS SAFE

Understand that the intellectually curious people in your congregation—the doctors, the engineers, the scientists, the philosophers—are probably keeping their doubts quiet, not because they don't have faith, but because they've learned that churches don't welcome hard questions.

You have an opportunity to change that. It won't be easy, but it's necessary.

Create regular spaces where questions are actually welcome. Set aside time—monthly, quarterly, whatever works—where people can ask anything about faith, theology, science, suffering, or doubt. Don't require that questions be submitted in advance for screening. Answer real-time questions from real people.

Here's the key: Answer them honestly. If you don't know, say so. If the question has multiple Christian perspectives, present them. If there's genuine tension that can't be easily resolved, acknowledge it. Don't pretend the church has everything figured out.

Bring in diverse voices, not just the pastor's. Invite scientists, doctors, theologians, counselors—people who can address questions from multiple angles. Show your congregation that brilliant Christians engage with these questions seriously.

Preach sermons that acknowledge complexity. Stop preaching like you have it all figured out. People can sense when you're being inauthentic, and nothing pushes thinking people away faster than a leader who pretends to have no struggles or doubts. Talk about the passages that confuse you. Share the times your faith felt shaky. Name the questions that still challenge you. Model what it looks like to have mature faith that includes mystery and uncertainty.

When you address hard topics—suffering, science, doubt, evil—don't offer simple formulas. Engage with the actual tension. Show your congregation that it's okay not to have everything resolved. Give people room to disagree without making them feel like heretics or second-class believers.

This doesn't mean preaching without conviction; it means preaching with humility. It means recognizing that God is bigger than your understanding and you're all still learning together.

Develop mentorship relationships intentionally. Pair people who are wrestling with questions with people who've wrestled with similar doubts and come through with their faith stronger, not people who will defend doctrine. Find people who will walk alongside, listen without judgment, and share their own journey honestly. This matters: Match people thoughtfully. Someone struggling with how science and faith fit together needs a mentor who understands both worlds. Someone processing grief after loss needs someone who's been through similar suffering. Someone questioning core beliefs needs someone secure enough in their own faith not to panic.

These relationships take time. Real wrestling takes time. Trust takes time. Don't expect a six-week program to do what only genuine relationships can do.

Build a resource library for questions. You don't need a staff theologian or scientist to do this. Create a library—physical or digital—that includes books, podcasts, articles, and videos on faith and science, suffering and theodicy, doubt and belief, church history and theology. Include diverse voices. Show people that Christians have been wrestling with these questions for centuries. Show them that brilliant, faithful people hold different perspectives. Don't pretend there's only one Christian answer to complex questions.

When someone is wrestling, point them to your resources about where other thoughtful people have wrestled too.

Train your leaders to listen first. Your staff, elders, small group leaders, and volunteers need to understand something: questions are usually signs of engagement, not rebellion. Someone asking hard questions is someone still thinking about faith. That's good.

Teach them to listen first, to ask clarifying questions instead of immediately defending or correcting. Help them see that their role is to create a safe space, not win arguments.

When a leader shuts down a question about how the Bible and science fit together, they're not protecting faith. They're teaching people that faith can't handle scrutiny. Train your leaders to do better.

Make doubt a normal part of your community's conversation. Create space for people to share their struggles publicly—in testimonies, in small groups, in the pulpit. Include the mess, not just the victory. Form small groups where people can be honest about doubts without fear of being reported to leadership or labeled as spiritually weak.

When someone says, "I'm wrestling with whether I still believe this," treat it like a normal part of faith. Check in. Offer support. Don't panic. Trust that God is big enough to handle their doubt and that wrestling often leads to deeper, more resilient faith.

This changes your whole culture. When people see doubt being treated as normal instead of catastrophic, everything shifts.

THE PAYOFF

This is how you stop losing the thinkers, the questioners, the doubters. This is how you build churches where people can bring their hardest questions about suffering, where curious kids can ask about science and faith, and where mission workers can engage honestly with people asking why Christianity matters.

Churches that make room for questions aren't weaker, they're stronger. They're more honest. They're more faithful to a God who invites us to seek, to knock, to ask, and who promises that those who seek will find.

The question is whether we are brave enough to open the door.

DISCUSSION QUESTIONS

1. Derrick grew up caught between his science teacher's persuasive lessons and his CRE teacher's rigid approach. How was faith presented to you growing up—as something that invites questions or something that demands unquestioning acceptance?

2. Caleb struggled with God's existence after his father's death. How does your church create space for people wrestling with suffering and doubt?

3. "The church has a problem with doubt and questions." Do you agree? When have you felt unsafe asking a hard question in your Christian community?

4. The author argues that "faith and reason aren't enemies; they're partners." How have you seen faith and intellectual curiosity work together in your life? Where have they seemed to conflict?

5. Think about the doubters and questioners in your life. What do they need most from you: answers, space to wrestle, or something else?

6. What question about faith do you have that you've been afraid to voice? What would need to be true for you to feel safe asking it?

7. Review the "What Churches Can Do" section. If you could implement one change to make your church more question-friendly, what would it be?

CHAPTER 3

THE CULTURAL BARRIER

"It's not just about me," he told me. "My faith is tied to my family, my community, my identity."

Early in my Christian faith formation, I started to develop friendships with people from different religions. One of these friends was Umaru, a Muslim gentleman in his late thirties. Although he was almost double my age, we grew very close, and he was like an older brother to me. For as long as I knew him, Umaru was always a very calm person with a steady demeanor and a unique and generous way of listening that always made me feel appreciated. Whenever I was going through hardship, I always found myself taught and mentored through every step, and he did it with compassion and profound understanding. During his spare time, we always went to watch soccer matches together, and he loved to talk about life with me.

As with many of my conversations with Umaru, these, too, gravitated toward the subject of religion. He was interested in Christianity, so I shared my testimony and explained different biblical concepts to him. He raised questions on grace, Jesus, and the concept of salvation itself. While wanting to know more about Jesus, Umaru was not ready to entertain the idea of converting. He revealed to me that his family, in particular his father, would be very harsh toward him if he were to leave Islam. Umaru was curious about the gospel, but the weight of his family's expectations kept him from moving forward. It is sobering to think about the extent to which culture and family create barriers to faith.

What I learned through our friendship is that I needed to be respectful and patient when spreading the gospel. I came to the conclusion that faith is very personal, and I could not impose my beliefs on Umaru. My only option was to remain his friend, pray, and live in a way that showed him Jesus. With Isma, things were different.

ISMA'S JOURNEY

Isma is a friend of mine with a story that sobers the heart while simultaneously lifting the spirit, and is one I shall cherish for a long time. He hails from a Muslim family and, like most Muslims, was deeply ingrained with the multicultural traditions, beliefs, and teachings of Islam. His parents, siblings, and the rest of his family were practicing Muslims, and like any child, Isma was expected to align his values with theirs. His family and community were pious and life was filled with prayers, Quran recitation, and various Islamic practices.

Having faith was a significant part of his life, to the extent that it defined his identity. It shaped every piece of his existence, from his family's status to the societal model he abided by. To him, faith was not merely traditions to be practiced. Like Umaru, it was a way to live life.

Nevertheless, though Isma was deeply devoted to Islam, he had one out-of-the-ordinary passion: soccer. It was on the soccer field where he started to have a taste of true freedom, genuine happiness, and expression of self unbounded by religious customs. It was also on the field that he met someone who, later in life, had a significant impact on his life—Jacob, who was a Christian. Isma, like many others, did not notice or care about their differences in faith because Jacob was just another teammate he would play the game with. With the passage of time, however, Isma started noticing things about Jacob. For one, Jacob did not treat the game as many other players did.

Isma noticed kindness in him, a sense of integrity and humility that was extremely rare. Also, Jacob treated all people with respect, irrespective of their background. There was something about his character that set him apart. While he was not forceful about his beliefs, he exhibited a quiet strength. This, my friend found very appealing.

Gradually, their talks expanded past soccer. Isma, who was never keen on religious debates, became interested in how Jacob lived. During one post-practice chat, he finally wanted to know what set Jacob apart from the other players. Without hesitating, Jacob shared the gospel, telling the young man about the love Jesus had, His grace, and how one could be saved through Christ. He said Jesus's love was sacrificial and not about rules and rituals but about a relationship with God. While he was speaking, Isma felt something within him change, a yearning for something more, something he had to pursue.

Isma knew that trying to pursue Christianity was extremely dangerous. Deep Islamic roots made it nearly impossible for him to entertain the thought of changing his religion. Regardless, the more he reflected on what Jacob shared, the more he became convinced of it. It dawned on him that his desire to learn more about Christianity was not simply an interest but a true desire. It dared him to change the way he viewed life.

Isma secretly started to read the Bible that Jacob had gifted him. At night, he snuck into his room, pulled out the Bible hiding under his mattress, and read during the still, silent hours, when he could lose himself in the Bible without the risk of being found out. As he continued reading, his comprehension of Jesus deepened. He started to view Jesus not merely as a historical character from a religion but also as the Redeemer who freely offered love, forgiveness, and a transformed life. He also started to understand that the more he read the Bible, the more he understood that the thing his heart was craving for was a personal relationship with God.

After months of secretly reading and praying, Isma thought the time was right to make a decision. With the help of Jacob, he underwent the rites of passage of visiting a Christian church. There, he accepted Jesus into his heart and was overwhelmed with unexplainable peace and joy. Soon after, he was baptized.

Unfortunately, the decision he made cost him more than he presumed. One day, when his younger sibling was playfully bounding on Isma's bed, the mattress jolted and exposed the Bible Isma was attempting to conceal. Out of curiosity, his younger sibling picked up the book and identified it almost instantly as not belonging to the set of religious texts held dear by the family. Without a second thought, he dashed toward their father to disclose the discovery he had made.

The consequences were immediate and catastrophic. Isma's father, enraged and grief-stricken over his son's choice to leave Islam, went to his son in anger, disbelief, and, most importantly, disappointment. He was determined to force a reversal of the decision Isma had made. He ordered him to convert back to Islam, but his son was resolute. He had made a choice and there was no turning back. His faith had grown, and he was willing to embrace the consequences. After the father's fury peaked, Isma was cut off completely. His father made it clear that he had no reason to come back home unless he decided to change his Christian beliefs and embrace Islam again.

Isma's heart broke as he was made to leave his family. The warmth of affection he had grown to appreciate within the family had now transformed into disapproval and shunning. But like many Christians in challenging situations, he had to follow Jesus at any price. "Whoever loves father or mother more than me is not worthy of me," is noted in Matthew 10:37. Jesus knew the cost. In the same breath, He said, "I have come to set a man against his father" (v. 35). But notice that He didn't say these words to push people away. He spoke them to prepare His followers for the reality that the kingdom often divides before it unites, and that following Him might mean standing alone before you find a new family. Isma's story reflects this verse and speaks to the cost of discipleship.

This young man later became a pastor. While his story is inspiring, serving as a testimony to the power of faith, it also speaks to the staggering cost of following Jesus. This recalls the words of Jesus in Luke 9:23, "If anyone would come after me, let him deny himself and take up his cross daily and follow me." Jesus promised Peter, "There is no one who has left house or brothers or sisters or mother or father or children or lands, for my sake and for the gospel, who will not receive a hundredfold now in this time, houses and brothers and sisters and mothers and children and lands, with persecutions, and in the age to come eternal life" (Mark 10:29–30). Isma lost his family, but he found a new one. The church became what Jesus promised: a hundred mothers, fathers, brothers, and sisters who chose him when his blood family wouldn't.

It was easier for me as I did not have to give up my family after making a decision to follow Christ.

MY OWN CULTURE

Growing up with my grandmother meant that I was exposed to the norms and values of Catholicism from my early childhood. Her impact is vivid in my memory. She emphasized the value of faith in our lives, the importance of devotion, and Catholicism's traditionalism. I recall the daily prayers, observances of our holidays, and collective family spirit during these cherished moments. She would tell me the deeds of saints and amaze me with miracle tales, instilling awe in me. She transformed Catholicism from a mere religion into a way to be, and I readily adopted her lifestyle. I was delighted with my tradition. Even as a small child, I experienced a strong attachment to our practices and the faith we professed. It is challenging to contemplate that someone back then might try to tell me my faith was incorrect, especially since those were the only beliefs I was raised with.

With the passage of time, I noticed inconsistencies in my relatives' belief systems, especially those of my father's side of the family. They practiced certain cultural traditions, like witchcraft and various superstitions, that were accepted in my family, but they were staunchly opposed to the teachings I received at home. Most of my relatives practiced these customs with the same fervor that people of faith practice their religion. To perplexed young boys like me, people whom we looked up to and considered idols were subscribing to ideas that were completely at odds with the teachings of the family. How could these people who educated me about faith accept both God and these so-called supernatural powers?

I found myself at the convergence of two opposing cultures: one that deeply cherished the Catholic religion, and one that held dear cultural traditions and customs I couldn't completely make sense of. While I was open to both sides of the argument, my faith was stifling, and I straddled two worlds of belief that made it impossible for me to settle on one. One thing, however, stood out across all these different beliefs: they all believed in a form of a higher, supreme power. Through the Catholic God I was taught about, or the various supernatural forces my relatives believed in, it seemed like everyone agreed there was something greater than ourselves. That acknowledgment of God is what held me steady.

I was confused, yet I eased my way onto the path my family had outlined. I fully accepted the Catholic traditions and their teachings, but all the while, I harbored a certain skepticism about who and what to believe. These differences fueled a desire I could not pinpoint. What I did not know was that these questions of mine were the first steps toward a transformative experience while at a gospel crusade, and a subsequent conversion to nondenominational Christianity.

FAITH AS FAMILY, CULTURE, AND IDENTITY— NOT JUST BELIEF

We in Christian churches have reduced a relationship with God to a decision. We've made it conditional—pray this prayer, sign this card, raise your hand, walk this aisle, and you're in. We treat conversion like flipping a switch: one moment you're not a Christian, the next moment you are. Simple. Clean. Individual. But for most of the world, faith doesn't work that way.

When Umaru told me his beliefs were about more than just himself, he was naming something we in individualistic cultures often fail to understand. For him, and for billions of people around the world, faith isn't just a personal belief system you can swap out like changing clothes. It's woven into the fabric of who you are, how you're known, where you belong, and what your future looks like.

To leave Islam wouldn't just mean Umaru changes what he believes about God. It would mean betraying his father, shaming his family, losing his community, and becoming an outsider in the only world he'd ever known. That's not just a spiritual decision. That's social suicide. Isma understood this cost intimately.

We read Isma's story and we're inspired by his faithfulness, his courage, his willingness to count the cost and pay it anyway. And we should be. His story is remarkable. But we need to sit with how rare it is. We need to understand that for every Isma who makes that impossible choice, there are hundreds, maybe thousands, of Umarus who can't. Not because they don't believe, not because they're not drawn to Jesus, but because the cost is simply too high.

And here's what we miss when we reduce faith to individual decision-making: we judge them for it. We think, *If they really believed, they'd leave everything and follow Jesus, just like the disciples did.* We question their sincerity, their commitment, their salvation. We make it a test of faith when really it's a collision of two completely different worlds.

I grew up caught between worlds myself. What I didn't understand then was that culture doesn't just disappear when you become a Christian. Culture is the water you swim in, the air you breathe. It's how you understand family, how you process grief, how you celebrate joy, how you make sense of the world. And when Christianity comes from the outside—often from the West and packaged with Western culture—people are forced to choose between Jesus and their identity. Between the gospel and their grandmothers. Between salvation and everything that makes them who they are. This is why so many people aren't Christians—not because they haven't heard the gospel, not because they don't find Jesus compelling, but because accepting Christianity feels like they are erasing themselves.

THE CULTURAL BARRIER

In many cultures, religion is corporate, not individual. You're not just choosing for yourself; you're also choosing for your children, for your family's reputation, for your place in society. In some contexts, converting to Christianity means your daughters won't be able to marry. Your business partners will no longer trust you. Your village will see you as a traitor. Your parents will mourn you as if you had died.

Jesus knew this. He said, "I have come to set ... a daughter against her mother, and a daughter-in-law against her mother-in-law. And a person's enemies will be those of his own household" (Matthew 10:35–36). He knew that following Him would cost people everything, including their families. But we forget that Jesus didn't condemn people for struggling with that cost. He didn't rush them. He didn't pressure them to make a decision before they were ready. He met them where they were and invited them to follow. And when the rich young ruler walked away sad because the cost was too high, Jesus didn't chase after him or question his faith. He let him go and grieved the heaviness of the choice (Mark 10:17–22).

We need to learn from that. We need to understand that for many people, coming to faith isn't a moment; it's a journey. And it might be a long one. It might involve years of secret Bible reading, like Isma. It might involve decades of friendship and questions, like Umaru. It might involve navigating impossible family dynamics, like I did growing up between my grandmother's Catholicism and my relatives' cultural practices.

Christian churches have done tremendous damage by treating evangelism like sales and conversion, like closing a deal. We count decisions instead of making disciples. We pressure people to make immediate commitments without understanding what those commitments will cost them. We treat faith as if it's merely intellectual assent to certain propositions, when for most of the world, it's about belonging, identity, and survival.

Despite having lost touch, I think about Umaru often. I wonder if he ever did come to faith. I wonder if the years of our friendship, the conversations we had, the soccer matches we watched together, planted seeds that grew in ways I never saw. I hope so. But I also know that I couldn't force it. I couldn't guilt him into betraying his father. I couldn't make light of what it would cost him to follow Jesus.

People from collectivist cultures and other religions, and people whose identity is wrapped up in their family and community, need time. They need space. They need us to honor the weight of what we're asking them to consider. They need us to stop treating evangelism like a contract and start treating it like what it is: an invitation into a completely new way of being in the world. And sometimes, that invitation takes a lifetime to accept.

WHAT CHURCH MEMBERS CAN DO: BUILD AUTHENTIC RELATIONSHIPS ACROSS FAITH

First, if you're trying to convert someone, stop. That's not friendship. That's a sales pitch disguised as relationship.

I learned this through Umaru. I could have spent our entire friendship waiting for the moment to "close the deal." Instead, I watched soccer with him. I talked about life with him. I let him mentor me through hard times. And yes, we talked about faith because that's what friends do. They talk about what matters most to them. But the faith conversations happened naturally, within genuine relationship, not as a strategy.

Build real friendships without an agenda. Befriend people who don't share your faith, not as a project or a stepping stone to conversion, but as actual friends. Care about their whole life—their work, their family, their dreams, their struggles. Invest years, not weeks. Be okay with the fact that you might pour into someone for a decade and never see them convert.

With Umaru, I stopped trying to convince him and started actually knowing him. I asked about his life. I listened to his concerns. I respected his hesitation about what conversion would cost him. I didn't minimize it or spiritualize it away.

Your job isn't to convert anyone. Your job is to love them well. Point them to Jesus. Then trust that God is doing what you can't.

Honor their culture while exploring faith together. Don't treat someone's culture as an obstacle to the gospel. Culture is how they understand the world. It's how they find meaning and belonging. Some aspects of their culture align with Jesus. Some don't. But the goal isn't to strip it away; it's to help them see how Jesus transforms it from the inside.

Ask questions instead of making pronouncements. "What does your culture value most?" "What does family mean in your context?" "How do you understand honor?" Then explore together how Jesus speaks into those things.

Be honest about the cost. If someone from another faith background is interested in exploring Christianity with you, don't lie to them about what it might cost. Don't say it'll all work out fine. It might not. Conversion could mean losing their family. Losing their community. Losing their place in society.

But also show them they won't walk that road alone. If they need housing, help them find it. If they lose their job, help them find work. If their family disowns them, help them find new family. The early church understood this. They shared everything so that people who lost everything wouldn't be left with nothing.

Be patient with the journey. When people come to faith from other religious backgrounds, they often bring pieces of their old beliefs with them. That's normal, not failure. That's humanity. Discipleship takes time.

Don't condemn every inconsistency. Walk alongside them. Give them space to figure out what it means to follow Jesus in their specific context. The Holy Spirit will do convicting work. Your job is just to be present.

Celebrate their story respectfully. If someone makes the leap to faith, celebrate it. But do it quietly. Respect their privacy. Don't turn them into a trophy for your evangelism efforts. Don't parade their conversion around. Let them decide when and how to tell their story. They might need to keep it quiet for safety. They might want space to process privately. Honor that.

WHAT CHURCH LEADERS CAN DO: WELCOME PEOPLE FROM OTHER FAITH BACKGROUNDS

Most of the world doesn't think about faith the way many Christian churches do. When you invite someone from that kind of background to consider Christianity, you're asking them to potentially lose their family, their community, their place in society. That's not a small ask. And if your church doesn't understand that, you'll drive them away.

Stop measuring evangelism by decisions. The number of people who pray a prayer with you is not the metric that matters. What matters is whether you're building real, long-term relationships with people from other faith backgrounds. What matters is whether they feel welcome, safe, and supported.

Train your congregation to build friendships with people who don't share their faith—not transactional friendships, real ones. Make it clear that the goal isn't conversion, it's genuine relationship.

Be patient. This takes years. It might take decades. That's not failure. That's faithfulness.

Create spaces where people can explore without pressure. People from other faith backgrounds need to know they can ask questions about Christianity without being pressured to commit immediately, without being made to feel like they're betraying their family just by asking.

Offer small groups, Q&A sessions, one-on-one conversations where curiosity is genuinely welcome. Let them read the Bible without demanding immediate acceptance. Let them voice real concerns about what conversion would cost them. Don't minimize those concerns. Sit with them. Acknowledge their weight. Pray about them together.

Honor their culture as you point to Christ. Don't present Christianity as something that requires cultural erasure. Show people that Jesus transforms cultural principles from the inside, not that He destroys them.

Ask thoughtful questions. Learn what their way of life values. Learn what family means in their context. Learn their traditions. Then help them see how Jesus speaks into those things—not by replacing them, but by transforming them.

Make it clear that following Jesus doesn't mean abandoning their food, their music, their names, their way of relating to family. It means bringing all of who they are into submission to Christ. That looks different depending on who the person is.

Prepare for the cost and provide real support. Be honest about what conversion might cost them. Don't promise easy answers, but offer concrete support. If they lose their job, help them find work. If they're disowned, help them find housing. If they're cut off from family, become family to them. Act like the early church (Acts 2:44–45). Create that kind of safety net in your church. Pair new believers from other faith backgrounds with mentors who understand what they're going through. Connect them with others who've walked similar paths. Don't celebrate their conversion and then abandon them to figure out the aftermath alone.

Be patient with cultural blending. When people come to faith from other religious traditions, they often blend their old beliefs with their new faith. They might pray to Jesus but also consult traditional healers. They might believe the gospel but also maintain practices that don't align with Scripture. This is called syncretism, and many churches treat it like a problem to fix immediately.

But discipleship takes time. Don't condemn every inconsistency. Walk alongside them as they figure out what it means to follow Jesus in their specific cultural context. Teach Scripture. Model biblical living. Then trust that the Holy Spirit will do the convicting and transforming work at the right pace.

Advocate for religious freedom globally. Many people who want to explore Christianity live in places where conversion is illegal, and where they could be imprisoned, beaten, or killed. Your church has a responsibility to fight for their freedom.

Support organizations that protect persecuted Christians. Raise awareness about countries where religious conversion is a capital crime. Pray for believers in hostile contexts. Use your freedom and your voice to advocate for those who don't have either.

Celebrate without sensationalizing. When someone from another faith background becomes a Christian, celebrate it. It's a miracle. It's worth rejoicing over. But respect their humanity in the process.

Don't reduce them to "the former Muslim" or "the ex-Hindu." They're people, not props. They've made an incredibly difficult decision. They might need to keep it quiet for their own safety. They might want space to process privately before going public. Honor that. Let them decide when and how to tell their story.

THE HEART OF IT ALL

This is how we reach people for whom faith is family, culture, and identity. We slow down. We build real relationships. We understand the genuine complexity of what we're asking. We make space for the long journey. We support people through real costs. We trust God with the timeline instead of pressuring for immediate decisions.

We stop treating evangelism like a sales strategy and start treating people like the image-bearers they are—complex, deeply rooted in community, carrying histories and identities we may never fully understand.

And we remember our job isn't to convert anyone. Our job is to love well, to point faithfully to Jesus, and to walk alongside whoever is willing to take even one step toward Him, even if that step takes a lifetime.

DISCUSSION QUESTIONS

1. Umaru told Derrick, "It's not just about me. My faith is tied to my family, my community, my identity." How does this challenge the Christian church's understanding of conversion as an individual decision?

2. Isma's story is inspiring but costly. He lost his family when he became a Christian. How does your church support new believers who face severe consequences for their faith?

3. Derrick describes growing up caught between his grandmother's Catholicism and his relatives' cultural practices. When have you felt caught between faith and cultural identity?

4. "We've made Christianity feel like they're erasing themselves." In what ways has Western Christianity been confused with Christianity itself? What would it look like to separate the two?

5. The chapter discusses the patience required when people are navigating impossible family dynamics. Think of someone you know who's interested in faith but hesitant. What might patience look like for them?

6. How can churches "honor culture while pointing to Christ"? What's an example of this done well or done poorly?

7. If someone from another faith background visited your church this Sunday, what cultural barriers might they encounter that have nothing to do with the gospel?

PART II

THE WOUNDS THAT DRIVE THEM AWAY

CHAPTER 4

THE FAILING LEADERS BARRIER

Many leaders are wonderful, godly people who model the love and holiness of Jesus all the time. There are others who do not, and it can be devastating to find yourself under one.

A few years ago, there seemed to be some friction between my pastor and one of his church assistants, a misunderstanding that, in my view, was ripe for some remorse and fairness. The assistant, to his credit, recognized his role in the struggle and went to my pastor to offer an apology and ask for forgiveness. This was a moment that should have resulted in healing and reconciliation. It didn't.

My pastor played a pivotal role in my life, serving as a spiritual guide I greatly respected and admired. Rather than a mere church speaker, he was a shepherd who cared about the spiritual growth and welfare of his flock. His sermons were captivating. He applied the timeless lessons of the Bible in ways that felt relevant and transformative week after week. Through his teaching, I gained clarity not only about the promises of God but also about the life of faith I should be living.

He was, in all ways that mattered, my spiritual guide and counselor. In times of hardship, he was available to help me and offer biblical encouragement. The prayers he gave felt personal, as if he carried the weight of each member's joys and burdens in his heart. My pastor was an example of godly leadership. Looking back, my trust rested as much on his position as on the person he seemed to be. I accepted his integrity, his reputation for sound judgment, and his apparent love for Christ, the church, and his people as real. I placed my deepest confidence in someone I believed was worthy of it, never imagining that foundation could crack.

But what happens when someone's true self doesn't match the high expectations they set by their words? Being a pastor is a position of deep trust, and when the cracks start to show, the fallout can be devastating. Everything that once gave you a sense of order, support, and spiritual stability gives way to confusion and pain. The trust that has been built and nurtured now feels out of reach. The anchor you depended on suddenly feels like it's dragging you under instead of holding you steady.

The moment came during one of his sermons. This man in whom I had placed my deepest trust was saying, "Forgive, and you will be forgiven," essentially preaching the opposite of what he had done. He was letting the matter with his church assistant worsen, showing coldness to the assistant, and ultimately terminating their working relationship. I was deeply disappointed in him, and I couldn't understand how he could fail to embody such a basic Christian principle, especially when the other party was humbly extending an olive branch. It felt like everything he had taught me about living the faith was crumbling. If forgiveness, the crux of Christianity, could be so easily disregarded, how could I trust anything else he'd taught me?

Jesus told Peter to forgive seventy-seven times—a deliberately impossible number meant to communicate limitless grace.

When religious leaders demand from others what they won't practice themselves, they become exactly what Jesus condemned: those who "tie up heavy burdens, hard to bear, and lay them on people's shoulders, but they themselves are not willing to move them with their finger" (Matthew 23:4). I felt a mix of confusion, betrayal, and sadness. It wasn't about expecting him to be perfect. It was about integrity. I expected him to uphold the faith he preached, yet he was withholding the very grace he taught us to give. That expectation felt violated.

This incident was one of many that forced me to wrestle with hard emotions and difficult questions. This gap between what he preached and how he lived—something many suffer through in silence—pushed me to confront uncomfortable realities about leadership, faith, and humanity itself. And it didn't just happen to me.

WHEN A PASTOR FAILS EXPECTATIONS

A few years back, my friend Sarah went through a scandal that shook and tested her faith. Sarah was an active member of the worship team at her church, a wonderful vocalist with a passion for leading others into worship. Serving brought her joy, and singing was her way of glorifying God. Her zeal and commitment inspired not just me, but many others too.

Then it was discovered that the senior pastor was having an inappropriate relationship with a congregant. Word spread like wildfire through the church. Sarah was devastated. She had worked with the pastor for years and regarded him as a spiritual father. She described it as having the foundation of her faith broken like glass, with deep fractures around her core.

I still recall her calling me, sobbing. "How can someone preach so powerfully about holiness and integrity and fall into such sin?" Her pain was unmistakable. She dealt with troubling shame, grappling with if-only narratives as if she could have somehow changed the outcome.

Witnessing Sarah's pain was difficult. It broke my heart to think about how the scandal was impacting not only her but also the entire church. Attendance plummeted, gossip abounded, and the congregation questioned the true intentions of their leaders. It was an unfortunate reminder that although a church is meant to reflect Christ, its leaders are all too human and capable of inflicting great harm on those they're meant to serve.

Through the scandal, both Sarah and I had to confront the reality of reconciling our faith with flawed church leadership. It was a reminder that our faith must be in God, not humans, and a powerful lesson in seeking the Lord's peace and guidance in times of pain. God's restorative powers in the darkest circumstances are truly remarkable.

Church scandals don't just impact individuals like Sarah—they inflict a devastating toll on the church as a role model and on the reputation of Christianity as a whole. The other disturbing side of leadership is that leaders can abuse their power and hurt many.

SPIRITUAL ABUSE

I have seen the devastating effects of spiritual abuse up close. A dear friend, Simone, spent her childhood in a church whose leaders imposed suffocating control over every aspect of members' lives. The pastor created an environment where Simone believed her value to God depended exclusively on her behavior, and no matter how hard she tried, she never reached the impossibly high standards the church set. Her clothing choices, her hours of community service, and even her conversations were subject to careful observation and public correction. Whenever she felt uncertain or dared to question a doctrine, she was quickly shamed and labeled disloyal. Convinced that God's love hinged on her flawless adherence to the church's rules, the weight of their enforced conformity became unbearable.

Simone's leaders twisted Scripture into chains. They forgot or ignored that Jesus said, "Come to me, all who labor and are heavy laden, and I will give you rest. Take my yoke upon you, and learn from me, for I am gentle and lowly in heart, and you will find rest for your souls" (Matthew 11:28–29). Gentle. Humble. Rest. Those words describe nothing of what Simone experienced. When leaders trade Jesus's gentle yoke for crushing control, they've stopped representing Him.

In time, Simone made the decision to walk away from the church, weighed down by betrayal and spiritual exhaustion. The wounds from that season left her wary of any congregation or spiritual leader, damaging her faith. It was only later, after extended seasons of emotional and spiritual healing, that she could—with the help of a healthy and supportive Christian community—recognize the twisted theology and subtle manipulation that had shaped her experience. Through persistent prayer, guidance from mentors, and a renewed engagement with Scripture, she gradually separated her understanding of God from the guilt and shame that had been used against her. In that process, Simone began an authentic relationship with God, marked by freedom and deepening trust.

TYPES OF LEADERSHIP FAILURE AND THEIR IMPACT

Leadership failure in the church isn't a single phenomenon; it's a range of brokenness that manifests in different ways, each leaving its own kind of wreckage, and the exposure of it is growing. Public trust in the church or organized religion has gone down from 50 percent to 36 percent since 2002 for a reason.[6] Understanding these failures matters because we can't address what we refuse to name. We can't heal wounds we pretend don't exist. And we can't protect people from harm if we're unwilling to acknowledge how that harm happens.

My pastor's refusal to forgive wasn't as dramatic as Sarah's pastor's affair or as systematic as Simone's pastor's abuse. But it was still a failure—a quiet, deceptive one that eroded trust and contradicted everything he taught. Some leadership failures often go unaddressed precisely because they seem too minor to matter. But they do matter. They all matter. Because each one chips away at people's faith, at their ability to trust, and at their willingness to stay.

The Moral Failure

Most people think of "pastor scandal" as the affair, the embezzlement, the addiction that finally comes to light. Sarah's pastor fell into this category. The man was living a double life, conducting an inappropriate relationship while standing in the pulpit every Sunday. The hypocrisy was staggering.

Moral failures destroy trust. If they were lying about this, what else were they lying about? If they could compartmentalize

---

[6] Gallup, "Confidence in Institutions," *Gallup*, https://news.gallup.com/poll/1597/confidence-institutions.aspx.

their sin while preaching against it, what does that say about everything they taught us?

The Character Failure

This is subtler than moral failure but equally damaging. It's the leader who isn't caught in obvious sin but whose character contradicts their calling. The pastor who preaches love but treats people with contempt. The elder who teaches humility but demands to be honored. The worship leader who sings about grace but gossips viciously. The youth pastor who talks about integrity but lies to cover mistakes.

My pastor's failure fell here. He wasn't having an affair or stealing money. He was failing to embody the most basic Christian principle of forgiveness while standing in front of hundreds of people, hypocritically teaching them they had no choice but to forgive.

Character failures are insidious because they're often defended or minimized. "Nobody's perfect." "He's under a lot of stress." "She's doing the best she can." "You're being too judgmental." These rationalizations protect the leader at the expense of the wounded. They gaslight people into thinking the problem is their expectations, not the leader's behavior. But character matters. It matters that leaders' private lives align with their public personas. When they don't, they create cognitive dissonance that damages people's faith. If the person closest to God can't live out basic Christian principles, what hope do the rest of us have?

The Abuse of Power

Simone experienced this firsthand. Her pastor didn't commit a moral failure in the traditional sense—there was no affair, no financial scandal. Instead, he used his position to control, manipulate, and spiritually abuse his congregation. He created an environment where people's worth was tied to their performance, where questioning was treated as rebellion, and where control masqueraded as care.

Spiritual abuse is particularly damaging because it weaponizes faith itself. The very things that should bring freedom—Scripture, prayer, community—become tools of oppression. God's love becomes conditional. Grace becomes conditional. Belonging becomes conditional. Everything depends on meeting impossible standards and submitting to the leader's authority without question.

Leaders who abuse power often do so gradually, building systems that make their authority unquestionable. They isolate people from outside perspectives. They create cultures where loyalty to the leader is equated with faithfulness to God. They use Scripture selectively to support their control while ignoring passages that would challenge it. And they punish dissent swiftly and publicly, making examples of anyone who dares to question them.

The damage from spiritual abuse runs deep and lasts long. People like Simone carry wounds that affect every subsequent spiritual relationship. They struggle to trust any leader. They second-guess their own perceptions. They wrestle with shame that doesn't belong to them. They have to rebuild their entire understanding of God from the ground up because the version they were taught was twisted beyond recognition.

The Failure of Courage

Some leadership failures aren't about what leaders do but what they fail to do. These failures are often institutional rather than individual, but they're failures nonetheless. When leaders choose comfort over courage, when they protect the institution at the expense of the vulnerable, when they value appearances over truth, they fail. And their failure creates an environment where harm continues unchecked.

I've watched this play out repeatedly. A youth pastor credibly accused of inappropriate behavior with students gets quietly moved to another church. A worship leader known for emotional manipulation keeps his position because he's talented and replacing him would be difficult. An elder who bullies staff members faces no consequences because he's a major donor. The pattern is always the same: protect the leader, sacrifice the wounded, maintain the status quo.

This kind of failure teaches congregations that power matters more than character, that reputation matters more than truth, that some people are too important to be held accountable. It breeds cynicism and drives away anyone with a functioning conscience.

THE CUMULATIVE IMPACT

These failures don't happen in isolation; they compound. One pastor's moral failure makes people suspicious of the next pastor. One experience of spiritual abuse makes people wary of any authority. One instance of leadership protecting itself at the expense of the vulnerable makes people doubt every institution.

The damage spreads beyond the immediate victims. Children growing up watching their parents' faith shattered by pastoral failure absorb the message that leaders can't be trusted, that faith is fragile, that church isn't safe. Spouses watching their partners wrestle with spiritual trauma wonder whether faith is worth the cost. Friends watching others abandon church after being wounded by leaders start questioning their own involvement. And the world watches all of this and concludes that Christians are hypocrites, that the church is just another corrupt institution, that there's no power in the gospel to actually transform people. Every leadership failure hands ammunition to critics and builds walls between seekers and Jesus.

The tragedy is that these failures are preventable, though, because we're all human, we all sin, we all fall short. But many of these failures could be caught early, addressed appropriately, and prevented from causing widespread damage if we had better systems of accountability, clearer boundaries, healthier cultures, and more courage to address problems when they're small rather than waiting until they explode.

WHAT CHURCH MEMBERS CAN DO: PROTECT YOURSELF AND OTHERS

This can be hard, but if you see leadership acting in ways that harm people, staying silent is not loyalty. It's complicity. I know these are people you respect, often people you love, and that speaking up feels disloyal. It feels dangerous. But protecting someone's reputation at the expense of vulnerable people isn't what Jesus taught.

Recognize warning signs and speak up. Learn to spot unhealthy leadership patterns: leaders who isolate themselves from answering to someone, who demand unquestioning loyalty, who shame people who ask questions, and who cover up failures. When you see these patterns, you have a responsibility to raise concerns. Use whatever reporting system your church has. If your church doesn't have safe ways to report concerns, push for them. If leadership responds defensively instead of investigating, that's another warning sign.

I know it's tempting to stay quiet, to assume someone else will speak up, and to tell yourself it's not your place. But sometimes you're the only person in a position to say something, and sometimes your voice is the one that matters.

Hold leaders accountable through everyday choices. Don't enable bad behavior just because someone is talented or charismatic. Don't rationalize boundary violations or financial opacity. Don't participate in cover-ups or defend leaders when evidence of failure emerges. Character matters more than gifts. A brilliant communicator who treats people poorly is still harmful. A dynamic leader who abuses power is still dangerous. Don't let talent make you excuse the inexcusable.

Support those harmed by leadership failure. If someone you know has been wounded by a leader, believe them. Don't minimize their experience. Don't pressure them to forgive quickly. Support them in getting help, especially from counselors trained in spiritual trauma. Your loyalty should be to truth and justice, not to protecting someone's reputation. The person who was harmed deserves more support than the person who caused the harm.

Be part of changing the culture. If your church is struggling with accountability issues, don't just accept it. Talk to others about it. Support leaders who want to change things. Attend meetings about governance. Vote for change if your church has a voting structure. Being a member means being part of creating a healthier culture.

WHAT CHURCH LEADERS CAN DO: BUILD ACCOUNTABILITY AND PROTECT THE VULNERABLE

Most leadership failures in churches happen not because leaders are uniquely evil, but because systems are broken. No one is holding them accountable. No one is asking the hard questions. No one is saying no.

Your job as a leader is to build systems that make failure less likely and that protect people when it happens anyway.

Create accountability structures with real teeth. Most churches have boards that rubber-stamp decisions and protect the pastor at all costs. That's not keeping the flock safe. That's a loyalty club. Real accountability requires people outside the pastor's inner circle who are willing to ask him the hard questions and challenge his decisions. It requires actual authority, not just advisory roles.

Require regular, honest check-ins on personal and professional health. Not surface conversations like "How's your walk with God?" but real ones. What temptations are you facing? Where are you struggling? Create environments where leaders can admit they're struggling before they fall. For larger churches or influential leaders, consider outside accountability—people from other organizations who have no stake in protecting someone's reputation. Pride whispers that you don't need outside voices. Pride is usually what comes before a fall.

Establish and enforce clear boundaries. Many leadership failures start small—a boundary crossed here, a line blurred there. A leader meets with a congregant alone behind closed doors. A text message at 11 p.m. A counseling relationship that continues without oversight. These small violations create environments where larger ones become possible.

Set clear policies:

- When and where leaders can meet with congregants one-on-one
- Communication boundaries (no personal social media connections with youth, no late-night texts)
- Financial transparency and decision-making
- Time off and rest requirements
- What happens when someone violates a boundary?

Make these public. Enforce them consistently. Don't make exceptions for "trusted" leaders or high-capacity people. The more influential the leader, the more important the boundaries. Make accountability mean something. If someone violates trust or crosses boundaries, there must be real consequences. Not a slap on the wrist. Not a sabbatical and then back to business. Consequences that match the severity and protect people from further harm.

Train everyone in leadership—from pastors to Sunday school teachers—on recognizing and maintaining boundaries. Make it clear: boundaries aren't about distrust. They're about protection for everyone.

Create safe reporting pathways. People who witness leadership failure need a way to report it without fear of retaliation. Too many churches have no clear process, or the process requires going directly to the person being accused, which is absurd and dangerous.

Establish multiple reporting options. Different people or teams someone can approach, depending on who the concern involves. Make sure at least one pathway goes outside immediate leadership to prevent cover-ups. Take every report seriously. Investigate thoroughly. Protect the reporter. And be willing to bring in outside expertise—professional investigators, trained counselors, legal counsel—when needed.

Create a culture where speaking up is seen as faithfulness, not disloyalty. Reward people who have the courage to raise concerns. Don't punish them for disrupting the status quo.

Prioritize character over charisma in leadership. Churches often choose leaders based on gifts or charisma, then act surprised when character can't sustain what those gifts built.

Make character nonnegotiable. Look for evidence of humility, integrity, self-control, faithfulness in small things, healthy relationships, and a pattern of growth over time. Check with people who've known the candidate in different contexts—former churches, workplaces, family members.

Don't rush. The New Testament warns against laying hands on someone too quickly. Give people time to prove their character before giving them authority. And be willing to remove leaders who demonstrate character problems, even if they're gifted. Healthier, less impressive leadership is better than impressive, destructive leadership.

Support leaders proactively so they don't fall. Many leadership failures happen because leaders are exhausted, isolated, or overwhelmed. You pile responsibilities on them, expect them to be available constantly, pay them poorly, then wonder why they burn out or make catastrophic decisions.

Pastoral Burnout, 2021–2022

Percentage of Protestant pastors seriously considering quitting full-time ministry

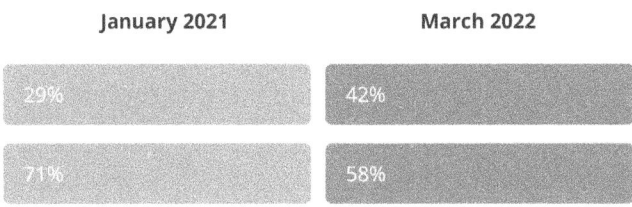

January 2021: 29% / 71%
March 2022: 42% / 58%

Figure 2. Primary reasons U.S. Protestant pastors considered quitting ministry in the past year (2021). Source: Barna Group, "Pastors Share Top Reasons They've Considered Quitting Ministry in the Past Year," April 27, 2022, https://www.barna.com/research/pastors-quitting-ministry/.[7]

Ensure your leaders have:
- Adequate compensation so financial stress isn't constant
- Reasonable work hours and mandatory time off
- Access to counseling outside the church
- Peer relationships with other leaders for support
- Clear job descriptions so expectations aren't infinite

Create a culture where leaders can be human, where they can admit struggle without losing their jobs, where asking for help is seen as wisdom, not weakness, and where rest is expected.

Respond to failure with both justice and compassion. When leadership failure happens, and it will, how you respond determines what happens next. Cover it up and you protect the

---

[7] Barna Group, "Pastors Share Top Reasons They've Considered Quitting Ministry in the Past Year," April 27, 2022, https://www.barna.com/research/pastors-quitting-ministry/.)

leader while traumatizing victims. Rush to restore the leader and you communicate that reputation matters more than people.

1. Prioritize victims. Believe them. Support them. Provide counseling. Remove ongoing threats to their safety. Make it clear that their healing matters more than the leader's reputation.
2. Investigate thoroughly. Don't rely on the leader's version. Talk to everyone affected. Get outside help if needed. Get to the truth.
3. Hold the leader accountable. This might mean removal from leadership, professional consequences, and legal action if laws were broken. The consequence should match the severity.
4. Communicate honestly with your congregation. Don't minimize what happened or protect reputation at the expense of truth. People can handle hard truths better than being gaslit.
5. Create space for grief. Congregations wounded by leadership failure need time to process, lament, and rebuild trust. Don't rush past the pain. There's no going back to "normal," only going through.

Care for the wounded long term. People wounded by leadership failure don't heal quickly. These wounds run deep. Provide access to counseling, especially from counselors trained in spiritual trauma. Create support groups. Check in regularly with those most affected—not just immediately after, but months and years later. Be patient with anger, doubt, and distance. These are normal responses to betrayal.

Don't pressure people to move on or forgive and forget. Healing can't be rushed. Trust, once broken, takes years to rebuild, if it can be rebuilt at all. Some people will leave your church. That's okay. Your job isn't to retain members; it's to love people well through their pain.

Learn and change. Every leadership failure is an opportunity to examine your systems. What allowed this to happen? What warning signs were missed? What policies need to change? What culture enabled this?

Be willing to make hard changes. Restructure if needed. Replace leaders who enabled the failure. Overhaul inadequate policies. Bring in outside consultants to see the blind spots you can't. Be transparent with your congregation about what you're learning. Show them you're taking this seriously and working to prevent it from happening again.

THE HEART OF IT ALL

Leadership failure doesn't have to be fatal to individuals or to congregations. When you take accountability seriously, establish clear boundaries, support leaders proactively, and respond to failure with both justice and compassion, you create environments where leaders are less likely to fail and where failure causes less damage when it happens.

This is how you protect vulnerable people. This is how you build churches where power doesn't corrupt, where the vulnerable are protected, and where failure is addressed rather than covered up.

Find the courage to do it.

BRIDGES NOT BARRIERS

DISCUSSION QUESTIONS

1. Derrick watched his pastor preach about forgiveness while refusing to forgive. When have you witnessed a gap between what a leader taught and how they lived?

2. Sarah's story about her pastor's affair shows how scandals affect entire communities. If you've experienced or witnessed a leadership scandal, how did it impact your faith? How did the church respond?

3. Simone experienced spiritual abuse through suffocating control. What's the difference between healthy spiritual authority and spiritual abuse? What are the warning signs?

4. The chapter distinguishes between moral failure, character failure, abuse of power, and failure of courage. Which type of leadership failure do you think is most common? Which causes the most damage?

5. "Every leadership failure hands ammunition to critics and builds walls between seekers and Jesus." How have you seen this play out? What responsibility do we have to address failures transparently?

6. Review the accountability structures in your church. Are they real or cosmetic? Who has the authority to challenge the senior leader if needed?

7. The author writes, "Some people will leave your church and that's okay." Do you agree? When is it right to prioritize truth and healing over retention?

CHAPTER 5

THE BARRIER OF EXCLUSION

"How can you say I might not even be a Christian?"

Politics divides families, churches, friendships, even among Christians, especially when your choices don't align with what your family or friends expect. My faith shapes how I see the world, but it also gives me room to make my own political decisions, even if they spark disagreements.

My family, whose values and standards can be called Christian in their essence, always seemed to be in conflict with whatever I chose to do in life. I found it somewhat peculiar, a paradox that, no matter how nonreligious they were, they still managed to hold me accountable to Christian values.

I've seen this same tension in churches. Friends have shared how they felt pushed out of congregations for supporting certain candidates or parties. They were labeled "not Christian enough," and some left their churches because they no longer felt welcome. One comment I saw online hit me hard: "You can't be a Christian and vote for the _____ Party. Jesus will vomit lukewarm Christians out of his mouth."

When those outside the church see our visible infighting, they rightly accuse us of hypocrisy and use it as a reason to stay away from Christ. I once overheard a coworker say, "If Christians can't even get along with each other, why would I want to join them?" Even back in 2007, a study of 16–29-year-olds found that they think "present-day Christianity is … too involved in politics (75%)."[8] Imagine what they'd say in 2025!

ENGAGING WITH OTHERS

Frequently, when we only connect with people who look like us or think like us, we create safe spaces that keep us from stepping outside what we already know. These spaces give us comfort and stability, but they also limit our ability to engage with people whose lives, habits, or perspectives are different from ours. Looking back, I realize I lived in one of these spaces my whole life without knowing it, until I started meeting people who carried different stories.

I remember noticing the accents of outsiders who came to my hometown, then asking them how they adjusted to our way of life. Their stories of struggle and adaptation seemed touching but distant, protected as I was by the familiar sounds of my own community. The moment I left and crossed borders, however, everything became real: I was the one whose voice marked me as out of place, and only then did I understand the weight carried by every word's pronunciation I couldn't control.

Traveling to nearby countries, I got used to the constant question about where my accent was from. At first, I took it as

---

[8] Barna Group, "A New Generation Expresses its Skepticism and Frustration with Christianity," *Barna*, September 21, 2007, https://www.barna.com/research/a-new-generation-expresses-its-skepticism-and-frustration-with-christianity.

THE BARRIER OF EXCLUSION

simple, polite curiosity. But the repetition began to mean something more: the realization that I would never quite blend into the local scene. This persistent, friendly question marked me as different and quietly planted the feeling that the city—the country—was drawing lines. The issue was no longer just pronunciation or vocabulary; it was my entire identity being questioned. Moving through this awareness, I discovered how hard it is to occupy a space when every part of who you are, from speech to body language, stands out. The uncomfortable recognition followed me.

When I relocated to the US and found my new church, my first goal was to find the young adult group. I thought that being around people my age would help me feel at home faster. I put the next meeting on my calendar. Walking into that gathering, though, brought a different reality: I was the only Black person in the room. The smiles and genuine questions directed at me were completely sincere, but the absence of anyone who shared my complexion, my background, or the unspoken understanding I found in other Black faces made the room feel too big for easy belonging.

I started to wonder if I would find my place here, if the church would truly feel like home. The thought of returning to the next meeting already felt daunting, but I believed that God, in His quiet faithfulness, was already preparing a path. The church brought in a new pastor for the young adult group, and, surprisingly, he was a Black man. For the first time, I saw a leader whose skin reflected mine, and that small thread of visibility drew me back. The similarity, minor when compared to everything else, shifted the entire dynamic.

My continued involvement in the group allowed me to build deeper connections with people whose life experiences were very different from my own. Over time, the initial discomfort faded, revealing the incredible value embedded in those very differences. Friendships formed in those hours have lasted, companions I now consider chosen family.

"YOU DON'T BELONG" MESSAGES

The church is supposed to be a place where everyone belongs, where the outcast finds family, the broken find healing, and the lost find home. But politics has become one of the most divisive forces in the modern church. I've watched churches split over elections. I've seen families stop speaking to each other because of who they voted for. But when did Jesus ever make our citizenship in His kingdom dependent on our political affiliation in an earthly one?

The truth is, faithful Christians have always held different political views. They've approached issues of government, economics, and social policy from various angles, all while loving Jesus and seeking to honor Him. But we've lost the ability to hold space for that tension. Instead of saying, "We can disagree and still be family," we say, "If you disagree with me, you must not really know God." That's not unity. That's conformity dressed up as belief.

Sexuality has become another line we've drawn in the sand. Now, let me be clear—I'm not suggesting we abandon biblical teaching or compromise on truth. But there's a difference between holding to Scripture and weaponizing it. There's a difference between speaking truth and using it as a club to beat people away from the very Savior they need.

I've seen people walk into churches carrying shame and questions about their sexuality, hoping to find grace, only to be met with condemnation before they even sit down. I've watched as churches made it clear that certain struggles are acceptable to bring to the altar, but others make you unwelcome at the door. We've created a hierarchy of sin that Jesus never endorsed. Somehow, we've decided that sexual sin is worse than gossip, that questions about identity are more dangerous than pride, that people wrestling with same-sex attraction are a threat, while people wrestling with greed can serve on the board of elders.

The message we send is clear: "You don't belong here unless you've already figured it out." But that's the opposite of the gospel. Jesus met people in their mess. He didn't wait for them to clean up before He called them. He invited them to follow Him, and the transformation happened along the way in community and through relationship.

Race is perhaps the most painful barrier because it often operates in silence. We don't always say out loud, "You don't belong because of your skin color." Instead, we communicate it through a thousand small actions. We communicate it when the only people in leadership are White. We communicate it when we ignore or minimize the pain of racial injustice. We communicate it when we make people of color feel like they have to assimilate—leave parts of themselves at the door—to be fully accepted.

I know what it feels like to walk into a room and realize you're the only one who looks like you. I know the exhaustion of wondering if you're welcome or just tolerated. I know the isolation of feeling like you have to explain yourself, your culture, your experience, over and over again, while others never have to think twice about whether they fit.

And here's what makes it even harder: when churches respond to these concerns with defensiveness instead of humility. When we say we don't see color, as if that's a virtue, when what we're really saying is, "We don't want to acknowledge your experience." When we call people "divisive" for naming the pain they feel, we prioritize our own comfort over someone else's dignity.

These barriers—politics, sexuality, race—all operate the same way. They all send the same message that there's an acceptable way to be a Christian, and if you don't fit that mold, you don't really belong. They take the expansive love of Jesus and shrink it down to fit their preferences, biases, and cultural moment. They make the gospel smaller than it actually is.

But the gospel is bigger than our politics. It's bigger than our discomfort. It's bigger than our homogeneous congregations. Jesus didn't die on a cross so we could build exclusive clubs. He died so that every barrier could be torn down—Jew and Gentile, slave and free, male and female. He died so that anyone, anywhere, no matter their background or struggle, could come home to the Father.

When we create these "you don't belong" messages, we're not protecting the church. We're betraying it. We're building walls where Jesus built bridges. We're closing doors He died to open.

WHAT CHURCH MEMBERS CAN DO

Challenge Exclusion in Your Community

It's hard to speak up when exclusion is happening around you. It's uncomfortable. It risks relationships. It makes people defensive. But silence is a choice, too, and it's a choice to let the exclusion continue. You have more power than you think to change the culture of your church.

Notice who's being excluded and why. Pay attention to who feels welcome in your church and who doesn't. Who speaks up in small groups? Who sits alone? Who leaves after a few visits and never comes back? Who visibly tenses up when certain topics come up? Start noticing patterns. Are people of color represented in leadership? Are people with different political views comfortable sharing their perspective? Are people asking questions about sexuality without fear? Are people from different socioeconomic backgrounds at ease?

When you notice exclusion, don't pretend it's not there. Don't tell yourself it's not your problem.

Speak up gently but clearly. If someone makes a political comment that assumes everyone votes the same way, you can say, "I actually see it differently." Not aggressively. Not to start a debate. Just to plant a flag that diversity of thought exists in your church. If you hear someone described in a limiting way, such as "They're struggling with their sexuality," said with judgment, you can simply respond: "I think they're a thoughtful person wrestling with real questions. I'm glad they're here."

If leadership only looks one way, you can ask in a board meeting or small group: "Have we thought about what message our homogeneous leadership sends to people who don't look like us?"

You don't have to be a hero. You just have to be willing to be a small voice for inclusion.

Invite people into belonging, not as a project, but as a person. If someone seems on the periphery, genuinely befriend them—not to fix them or integrate them into the "right" group, but to know them. Invite them to lunch. Ask about their life. Make space for them to be exactly who they are.

I almost didn't go back to that young adults' group because I was the only Black person there. But one person—the new pastor—saw me. He didn't pretend my difference didn't matter. He just let me know I mattered. That made all the difference.

Resist the pressure to choose sides. Churches are increasingly becoming echo chambers where you're expected to align politically, culturally, and theologically. Resist that. Maintain friendships with people who see the world differently. Show that you can disagree and still belong to the same family.

This is countercultural. The world wants you to choose a tribe and defend it fiercely. The church should be the one place where that's not required.

Advocate for change without being confrontational. If your church is becoming more exclusive, you don't have to be a martyr about it. You can quietly ask questions like, "Why don't we have more racial diversity in leadership?" and "What would it look like to welcome people who think differently about politics?" or "How can we create a place where LGBTQ+ people feel safe to bring their whole selves before God?"

Questions are powerful. They don't attack. They invite reflection. They can shift a culture without creating massive conflict.

WHAT CHURCH LEADERS CAN DO: DISMANTLE BARRIERS TO BELONGING

Understand that your church is sending messages about who belongs, whether you intend to or not. Everything from your leadership composition to what you emphasize in sermons to how you respond to certain topics communicates who's welcome here.

The question isn't whether your church is exclusive. The question is how exclusive you want to be.

Examine your leadership composition honestly. Look at who's making decisions in your church. Who's preaching? Who's visible in positions of authority? If everyone looks the same, thinks the same, votes the same, you're not reflecting the kingdom of God; you're reflecting your own tribe. This isn't about quota filling or tokenism. It's about actually believing that different perspectives strengthen leadership. It's about understanding that people of color need to see themselves in leadership to feel like they belong.

Ask yourself hard questions like: "Why don't we have racial diversity in leadership?" "What would we have to change to make that possible?" "What discomfort would we have to tolerate?" Then make deliberate changes, not in response to external pressure but because you've decided that exclusivity isn't acceptable.

Separate the gospel from your political opinions. Stop making voting records tests of orthodoxy. Stop implying that there's only one Christian way to vote on healthcare, immigration, economics, or any other issue. From your pulpit, make it clear: "In this church, you can be a thoughtful Christian and vote differently from me. In this church, we disagree on politics and we're still family." Then model it. Have leaders who disagree politically sitting next to each other. Show that disagreement doesn't mean disloyalty. Show that you can hold different political views and still love Jesus.

This is hard. Political tensions are real. But the church should be the one place where we prove that unity doesn't require uniformity.

Create genuinely safe spaces for people wrestling with sexuality. I'm not asking you to compromise on biblical teaching. I'm asking you to teach it with compassion instead of condemnation. Make it clear that people wrestling with sexuality, identity, or attraction are welcome in your church. Not welcome *if* they change, but welcome now. Create small groups where these conversations can happen without judgment. Train leaders to listen before they correct.

Stop treating sexuality as a hierarchy of sin while ignoring greed, gossip, or pride. If you're going to have standards, apply them consistently. If you're going to extend grace, extend it to everyone.

Build a racially diverse congregation intentionally. If your church is predominantly one race, ask why. Is it because that's who lives in your neighborhood, or is it because you've created a culture that only appeals to people who look like you? Examine everything: your music style, your leadership, your preaching illustrations, the stories you tell, the assumptions you make. Do they communicate that this is a space for everyone, or do they communicate "this is for people like us"?

Then make changes. Diversify your leadership, include different musical traditions, and tell stories from different cultural perspectives. Make it clear that this is a church that belongs to everyone. And don't just recruit people of color to fill seats, actually integrate them into community and leadership. Actually listen when they name barriers. Actually change things based on what you hear.

Respond to concerns about exclusion with humility, not defensiveness. When someone says, "I don't feel welcome here," your first instinct might be to defend: "We are welcoming! Everyone's welcome!" But that's not what they're telling you. They're telling you they felt excluded. Listen. Don't explain. Don't defend. Just listen.

If someone says the church is too political, don't argue about whether you were actually political. Ask: "What gave you that impression? What would make you feel more welcome here?" If someone says they didn't see themselves in leadership, don't say, "We don't see color." Ask: "What would help you feel like you belong?"

This is how you learn. This is how you change.

Make space for people to disagree without losing belonging. Create forums where different perspectives are actually welcome, panels on controversial topics where multiple Christian viewpoints are presented, and small groups where people can voice doubts safely without being labeled as difficult.

Make it clear that members can disagree with leadership and still belong, can question doctrines and still be part of the community, can struggle with core beliefs and you'll walk with them. This changes everything. When people know they won't be shamed for thinking differently, they stay. They engage. They grow.

Hold yourself accountable for becoming more inclusive. Don't just talk about inclusion, measure it. How many people of color are in leadership? How many people with different political views feel safe?

Ask uncomfortable questions in board meetings. Bring in outside consultants to assess your culture. Listen when people from marginalized groups tell you what barriers they experience. Then actually change things based on what you learn.

Celebrate diversity as strength, not tolerance. Don't frame inclusion as something you're doing for other people. Frame it as something that makes your church stronger. Different perspectives sharpen thinking. Different experiences deepen wisdom. Different backgrounds reflect the actual kingdom of God.

Make sure your congregation understands this. Preach about it. Celebrate it. Show that you genuinely believe that churches with diverse leadership, diverse perspectives, and diverse experiences are healthier, more faithful, and more aligned with Scripture.

THE HEART OF IT ALL

The gospel is bigger than politics, bigger than cultural comfort, bigger than our preferences about who should lead. Jesus didn't die to create exclusive clubs. He died to tear down every barrier.

Your job as a leader is to dismantle the barriers your church has built, not defend them. This is hard work. It requires humility, courage, and willingness to make insiders uncomfortable to make outsiders welcome.

But that's what faithfulness looks like.

THE BARRIER OF EXCLUSION

DISCUSSION QUESTIONS

1. Derrick describes walking into a young adults' group as the only Black person in the room. When have you been the "only" in a space? How did it feel?

2. "Politics has become one of the most divisive forces in the modern church." How has politics affected your church or Christian friendships? What would it look like to separate gospel from politics?

3. The chapter discusses sexuality as a barrier. How can churches hold to Scripture and speak truth, while also creating spaces where people wrestling with sexual identity feel genuinely welcomed?

4. "We've created a hierarchy of sin that Jesus never endorsed." What sins does your church treat as acceptable to struggle with, and which ones make people unwelcome? Why the difference?

5. Think about your church's leadership, both visible and behind the scenes. Who's missing? Whose voices aren't being heard?

6. The author challenges readers to examine their assumptions. What assumption do you hold about who belongs in church that you've never questioned before?

7. "Lead with love" is the chapter's core message. What would change in your interactions this week if you led with love toward someone whose politics, lifestyle, or questions differ from yours?

CHAPTER 6

THE BARRIER OF FILTERED FAITH

I met Daniel on the soccer field, where we enjoyed the rhythm of the game—running, kicking the ball, building strategies as we played. It always amazes me how sports quietly break down walls. We started as two players making passes, trading names and favorite teams between drills. Slowly, the small talk changed; jokes got deeper, and what had been a sideline conversation about formations turned into reflections on hopes, doubts, and occasional thoughts about mercy and judgment. Months later, the field still marked our shared space, but the conversations had grown into something like friendship.

Early on, I noticed something in Daniel I hadn't seen much in people I'd known before. He held an almost automatic skepticism toward anything religious, Christianity especially. When he talked about churches, pastors, or the Bible, it was clear he'd learned a story mostly from screens. These ideas hadn't come from sitting in a church or reading Scripture for himself. His manner wasn't hostile, but his words carried a soft finality, like he'd already decided the faith I follow wasn't worth exploring. I didn't take it personally, but it made me think about how much power media still has in shaping what we believe.

Daniel's parents had always seen formal religion as a polite social thing that didn't carry much weight. They accepted the Christian tradition with a shrug but never thought it addressed anything deeper than habit. So Daniel grew up outside any structured faith, free to form his own opinions, which he did, mostly alone. Popular media gave him images—loud evangelists on TV, cynical sitcom pastors, scandal figures asking for money. I remember him describing it one night after soccer. "Why is it that every Christian I see on a screen is either crazy or crooked?" he said, leaning back on the gym bench.

At first, I didn't push him on his views, but I soon noticed the overall impact of what he consumed online—a constant drumbeat of distrust toward religion. But one afternoon, his tone shifted to curiosity, not confrontation, and we moved toward the deeper subject of faith. He crossed his arms and asked,

"Why would I want to join a group that keeps fighting and judging everyone?"

I felt the distance between his question and my answer, but I spoke anyway, drawing a line between the headlines and the life I'd lived. I told him how the viral clips and trending memes magnified the bad moments of faith and forgot the good ones. The real story, I said, wasn't what showed up on church signs but what lived in the actual pages of the Bible—the man we call Jesus, who welcomed scandalous outsiders and never picked up a stone. "I don't fit a type," I said. "I'm trying to follow Him." I sensed the first small crack in his defenses.

"Wait," Daniel said slowly, "so you're not the poster child for judgment, the one who already knows I'm wrong?" The question hung between us, his tone barely holding back disbelief, leaning toward wonder. He looked at me like my life was a book he'd never opened.

THE BARRIER OF FILTERED FAITH

In that moment, I saw how Daniel had never encountered Jesus directly; he'd only encountered His distorted reflection. I didn't want to pressure him, but I pointed out that journalists usually focus on extremes—people who act in faith's name but in ways that go against Christianity's heart. I mentioned that Jesus Himself was misunderstood and misrepresented by the people around Him. I brought up Isaiah 53:3, which describes Him as "despised and rejected by men," yet He stayed faithful to His mission of love, grace, and sacrifice.

That conversation marked a small shift. Daniel didn't come to faith right then, but something had changed in him. In the weeks that followed, he started asking sharper questions. One evening, he asked,

"What's the difference between cultural Christianity and real Christianity?"

Daniel's journey unfolded slowly over the months, never rushed, always careful. He began to see the faith itself. Love, grace, and renewal started to matter to him on their own terms, not as the joke culture had sold him. Our ongoing conversations pushed him toward the gospel's beauty, not the distorted image he'd learned to reject.

"I see now how much of my opinion came from screens instead of the actual story," he said one night. "It's easy to mock what you never bothered to meet, especially when everyone around you is already laughing."

For Daniel, the turning point wasn't a new philosophy; it was a new set of experiences. He started sitting beside me in church, then came back week after week to a small group, where questions had space to exist. In that safe, open community, Daniel became convinced by the brightness of God's grace and compassion. Skepticism gave way to curiosity, and curiosity opened into a quiet but steady acceptance of the truth.

A FALSE FRONT

Digital media presents people in a false light, but it's not only social profiles that do this. I'll tell you about a friend I'll call Mark, whose arrival in the community I once served is still vivid in my mind. Before the gospel reached him, Mark's life was marked by addiction and betrayal. The night of his first, hesitant visit to the church, no lightning struck. He hid the truth of his struggles, convinced that the church had no room for people "like him." But the culture of that congregation was one where honesty was both normal and safe. Each time a brother or sister reminded him that yesterday's chains don't stop tomorrow's freedom, a small spark in Mark's heart grew brighter.

At some point, Mark decided he couldn't stay hidden anymore. He started letting people see him, letting them into his life, and he began reaching out for the help he'd kept at arm's length for so long. The pull of his old habits kept tugging at him, dragging him back just as he thought he'd made progress. But steady involvement in discipleship, the stable embrace of a caring church, and the ongoing guidance of mentors quietly redirected his path.

I can point to specific moments when God seemed to carve out new space in Mark, marking him through small victories—laying down a particular vice, choosing to forgive a fresh wound, speaking his heart in prayer for the first time. Gradually, the young man emerged as a solid presence in our youth ministry, celebrated not for perfect progress but for steady forward motion.

The power of confession in community is ancient. James wrote, "Confess your sins to one another and pray for one another, that you may be healed" (James 5:16). Not "confess to God alone in private." Not "fix yourself first, then join the community." Confess to each other. Healing happens in the light, in the presence of people who know your mess and choose to stay.

Mark's changed life sharpened my own view of God's patience and reminded me to extend the same to others. If God could use Mark's story to draw people to the Savior, then I began to believe God could use my imperfect story too.

People weren't only avoiding church because of shame though.

IT'S BORING

"Christianity is boring." This is something I've heard many times, especially from my non-Christian friends. I think of my childhood friend Stanley specifically. Although not a Christian, he's always been open to the gospel. We've had many discussions about faith, and each time I share the gospel of Jesus, he engages fully. However, no matter how much he engages, at the end of our conversations, he always says, "I believe in God, but I can't do Christianity. It's boring. I'm a party person and I can't follow all those life restrictions."

There are many people who think the way he does. But the question is: Is the way of life Christianity preaches actually boring, or is it simply a matter of it being misunderstood?

HOW VIRTUAL RELATIONSHIPS SHAPE FAITH PERCEPTIONS

We live in a world where most people's first encounter with Christianity doesn't happen in a church but on a screen. By the time they consider faith for themselves, they've already formed an opinion based on a curated, distorted version of what Christianity actually is.

This is Daniel's story, but it's also the story of millions. He'd never opened a Bible. He'd never had a real conversation with someone trying to follow Jesus. But he was convinced he knew exactly what Christianity was: either crazy or corrupt, fanatical or fake. And here's the thing—he wasn't being unreasonable. The version of Christianity that dominates online actually does look that way. Algorithms don't reward nuance or inaudible faithfulness. They reward outrage, spectacle, and controversy. So the Christianity that goes viral is the Christianity that yells the loudest, falls the hardest, or fits the most convenient stereotype. The result is that people like Daniel—people who've never stepped foot in a church—have a completely warped picture of what faith actually looks like.

Virtual relationships shape faith perceptions in powerful ways, and most of it happens without us even realizing it. Social media doesn't just connect us to people; it curates reality for us. It decides what we see, who we hear from, and which stories get amplified. And when it comes to Christianity, the stories that get amplified are rarely the good ones.

Think about how that's the Christianity they encounter. Not the single mom in their neighborhood quietly serving at a food bank. Not the couple fostering kids nobody else wanted. Not the friend who showed up at 2 a.m. when they were falling apart. Those stories don't trend. They don't go viral. They're too ordinary, too real.

But it's not just non-Christians whose faith perceptions are shaped by virtual relationships. It's us too. How many have written off entire denominations because of a viral clip taken out of context? We're all susceptible to this. We see someone's highlight reel and assume their life is perfect, or see their worst moment go viral and forget they're a whole person with a whole story. Virtual relationships flatten people into caricatures, and

THE BARRIER OF FILTERED FAITH

when we let those caricatures shape our understanding, we lose the ability to see each other clearly.

Here's what I've learned: The only antidote to digital distortion is real relationship. Daniel's view of Christianity didn't change because I sent him better articles or showed him inspirational videos. It changed because we became friends. Because he saw my life up close, not through a filter. Because he asked hard questions and I didn't have scripted answers. Because he came to church and met people who were messy and honest and still trying to follow Jesus.

Real relationship is slow. It's inconvenient. It doesn't scale the way a viral post does. But it's also the only thing that cuts through the noise. When someone knows you—actually knows you—they can't reduce you to a meme. They can't dismiss your faith as performance or delusion. They have to reckon with the reality of what they see in your life. This is why the early church grew the way it did, not because they had better marketing or more compelling content, but because they loved each other in ways the world couldn't ignore. "See how they love one another," people said. Not "see how they argue online" or "see how they cancel each other." They saw love, and it made them curious.

We need to recover that. We need to remember that faith is caught more than it's taught, and you can't catch it through a screen. You catch it in kitchens and coffee shops and soccer fields. You catch it when someone shows up for you, not because it's convenient but because that's what love does. You catch it when you see grace in action, not just in theory.

Virtual relationships will continue to shape faith perceptions. That's not going away. But we get to decide what shape they take. We can contribute to the noise, or we can offer something different. We can perform for the algorithm, or we can live authentically and let people see what following Jesus actually looks like.

WHAT CHURCH MEMBERS CAN DO: REPRESENT CHRIST ONLINE

Your life is the most powerful argument for Jesus that exists. Not your words. Your life. Daniel didn't come to faith because I won a debate with him. He came to faith because he watched my life over months. Because I showed up. Because he saw grace in action, not just heard about it in theory.

Stop performing your faith on social media. I know the temptation. You want to share the good stuff—the spiritual victories, the answered prayers, the profound insights. You want people to see your best self. But here's what happens: when all people see is your highlight reel, they conclude that Christianity is either fake (because nobody's life is that perfect) or impossible (because they can't measure up).

When Daniel saw my messy, imperfect faith, it became credible to him. When he met people in church who admitted their struggles, it felt like a place he could belong. Share your actual life. Show people what real Christianity looks like—not perfect, but genuine.

Build real relationships instead of collecting followers. Stop trying to influence large audiences and start actually knowing people. Deep friendships take time. They can't be rushed. They can't be scaled. But they're the only thing that cuts through the noise.

Form genuine friendships with people in your life. Be present. Be authentic. Let them see who you actually are, not who you're trying to be online.

Be honest about your faith struggles. Don't pretend you have it all figured out. Don't act like your faith is perfect or your walk with God is always steady. Talk about your questions. Share your doubts. Be real about the times you're struggling. This gives people permission to be real too. This shows them that you can wrestle with faith and still believe. This transforms faith from something you perform into something you actually live.

Engage with people where they are. If someone tells you they think Christianity is boring or that they only know Christians from what they see online, don't defend Christianity. Listen. Ask them what they've seen. Let them tell you what their perception is based on. Then, over time, show them something different, not through lectures or arguments, but through genuine friendship and authentic living.

WHAT CHURCH LEADERS CAN DO: COUNTER DIGITAL DISTORTION WITH REAL COMMUNITY

You can't control what people see about Christianity online, but you *can* build a real community that offers something different. You can create a place where people encounter actual Christians, not filtered versions.

Train your congregation to be authentic online. Most church members don't understand the power of their social media presence. They think they're just sharing their faith. They don't realize they're contributing to either the problem or the solution. Teach them: Don't just post victories. Share struggles. Don't just celebrate answered prayers. Be honest about unanswered ones. Don't just show your best self. Let people see your real self.

When Christians online are authentic—when they admit doubts, share failures, show imperfection—it changes the conversation. It counteracts the perception that Christianity requires perfection.

Make your church's online presence about authenticity, not marketing. Your website, your social media, everything represents your church online. What message are you sending? Are you trying to look impressive? Or are you trying to be honest? Are you curating an image? Or are you showing reality?

Post stories about messy faith journeys, not just success stories. Share about doubts people are wrestling with, not just certainties. Show people who are broken and still showing up, not just people who have it figured out. When someone looks at your church's digital presence and sees authenticity, it creates curiosity. It makes them think, *Maybe these people are real.*

Invite people into real community, not virtual community. Social media can introduce people to your church, but it can't transform them. It can't create belonging. It can't show them what real faith looks like. Use technology as a starting point. Then get people off their screens and into actual relationship.

Create spaces where people can meet in person—small groups, coffee hangouts, serve projects, sports leagues—places where they encounter real Christians being real with each other. That's where faith is caught, not from screens but from actual people in actual community, living actual faith.

Be radically honest about Christianity's failures online. When there's a scandal, don't hide it. When Christians behave badly, don't defend them. When the church gets it wrong, admit it. Some of the most powerful witness comes from Christians acknowledging failure and repenting. It shows that we're not trying to hide behind a perfect image. It shows that we actually care about truth more than reputation. This builds credibility in a world drowning in BS.

Show what real, ordinary Christianity looks like. The Christianity that goes viral is usually extreme—either incredibly inspiring or incredibly awful. But most Christians are just ordinary people trying to follow Jesus in their regular lives. Highlight that. Tell stories about the single mom cooking for a neighbor, or the couple taking in their son's friend, or the woman sitting with a church member during every chemotherapy appointment. These stories won't go viral. They won't get thousands of likes. But they're real. And they're the closest thing to what people are actually looking for.

Create spaces where people can ask real questions. If someone comes to your church with a warped view of Christianity learned from the internet, they need space to explore what actual Christianity is. Not to defend the faith against their criticisms, just to encounter it directly.

Create Q&A sessions where people can voice their objections. Create small groups where questions are genuinely welcome. Create one-on-one conversations where someone can say, "Everything I know about Christianity comes from the internet, and it all seems wrong." Then show them something different through real relationship.

Measure success by transformation, not engagement. Stop counting likes and shares and views. Start asking if people are encountering real faith. Are they being transformed? Are they moving from digital skepticism to a genuine encounter with Jesus?

This is slower. It's harder to measure. It can't be optimized the way viral content can be. But it's the only metric that actually matters.

THE HEART OF IT ALL

Digital distortion is real and powerful. But it's not more powerful than authentic community. When people encounter real Christians—imperfect, honest, genuine—living real faith in real community, the digital distortion loses its power. Your job as a leader is to build that kind of community. Not a community that performs perfection for social media, but a community where people can be real, where faith is lived out loud, and where grace is visible. That's how you counter the narrative, not with better marketing or more compelling content but with actual people, in actual relationship, living actual faith.

DISCUSSION QUESTIONS

1. Daniel's entire perception of Christianity came from screens—movies, social media, viral clips. What does the world see when they encounter Christianity online? Is it representative of Jesus?

2. Mark's story shows transformation through authentic community. Who in your life needs to see the real, messy, grace-filled side of Christian community instead of a filtered version?

3. Stanley says Christianity is "boring" and full of restrictions. How would you respond to him? What would you want him to see about the life Jesus offers?

4. "Virtual relationships shape faith perceptions in powerful ways." What's your own church's social media presence communicating? What would an outsider conclude about your community from what they see online?

5. The author writes, "Real relationship is slow. It's inconvenient. It doesn't scale the way a viral post does." When was the last time you prioritized a slow, inconvenient, real relationship over digital convenience?

6. Think about your own social media presence. Do your posts and interactions make people more curious about Jesus or more cynical about Christians?

7. How can your church use technology to build authentic relationships rather than just broadcast content? What would that look like practically?

PART III

BUILDING BRIDGES THAT LAST

CHAPTER 7

BEYOND SUNDAY PERFORMANCE

My childhood comes to mind in a series of nostalgic moments. Growing up in Uganda, my mornings consisted of the homely scent of chapati sizzling on the stove, with my grandmother humming to soft tunes in the background. To my young self, breakfast felt special—a sweet cup of tea and a slice of bread, lifting my spirits for the day ahead. I remember school as a walk along a dusty road lined with lush mango trees. The best summers consisted of breakfast, a few hours at school, then video games and a hearty snack. As the sun began to set, a simple dinner was followed by falling asleep. To my young, carefree self, life felt like there was no countdown, no timers, just days to enjoy. Each day was filled with possibilities.

Yet there's one thing I overlooked during that period of my life, and that is my faith. Even though I accepted Christ as Savior at an early age, I never really made Him the focal point of my life. During the daily flow of life, I tended to ignore His guidance, assuming the presence of my faith was enough. I was unaware of how vital it was to make a conscious effort and reserve at least a fraction of my day to talk to Him, even about the really small things.

I had my first taste of busyness in middle school, but high school brought its own crushing weight. Sent to a boarding school, the change felt more like going from a leisurely stroll to military boot camp. My waking hours were now filled to the brim with rigid schedules and a maze of rules to follow. Breakfast had to be quick, and by sunrise, we were already in class for reading sessions. Following those, formal classes ran until the first break at 10 a.m. My breakfast was capped at thirty minutes, providing next to no energy to last through the morning. Lessons resumed at 10:30 a.m., and before I knew it, lunch was on the horizon. My lunch break ended at 1:00 p.m. Classes resumed again and ran until 4:00 p.m., followed by a short dinner break.

Evenings granted us a maximum of two hours of "free time," which was quickly consumed by assignments, chores, and other obligations. Following this were the nightly study sessions, which went until 10 p.m. and consisted of reviewing class material or preparing for exams. The nightly sessions, coupled with everything else, resulted in a complete lack of leisure. Bedtime was yet another routine. This tight schedule was the complete opposite of comforting, and for the very first time in my life, I understood the meaning of the word "busy." Attending that boarding school truly taught me that time is a limited resource that requires complete optimization.

Throughout those challenging school years, I learned how easy it was for someone like me to forget about God in the midst of everything. I still identified as a Christian, but the constant strain made me feel burnt out, and my faith was relegated to a mere afterthought. I tried to go to church, but it was more of a formality. My relationship with God had taken a back seat to the demands of school. The more fixated I became on my to-do list, the easier it became to neglect the One who had always been there to guide me.

Looking back, I see now how busyness became my new religion. I worshiped at the altar of productivity. My worth became tied to how much I could accomplish, how well I could manage my time, and how efficiently I could check items off my list. God wasn't absent from my life—I still believed in Him, still thought of myself as His follower, but He was pushed to the margins, squeezed into whatever gaps remained after everything else was done. And there were never any gaps.

The irony is that I thought I was doing the right thing. I thought working hard, staying disciplined, and meeting every obligation was what responsible Christians did. I convinced myself that God understood I was busy and that He would be there when I had more time. But "more time" never came. The schedule never loosened. The demands never decreased. I just kept moving, kept grinding, kept telling myself that once this semester ended, once this year finished, I'd make space for Him again.

In the beginning, I imagined this grueling schedule was something I would endure only during high school. I had the notion that as soon as I graduated, I would once again have an easier and more relaxed life. Now, all these years later, I understand just how much that form of living shaped my life. My life now feels like a mirror of those boarding school days: wake up, work, take breaks, have lunch, continue working, head home, have a very short rest, sleep, and repeat the next day.

At first, I thought this was just the way life was and how people lived. With the passage of time, I started questioning it. Is this really the life designed for us by the Creator? Is life just a collection of rushing from one activity to the next, like some never-ending machine, churning without pause?

The truth I'm learning—slowly and painfully—is that busyness doesn't just crowd out time with God. It changes how we see Him. When we're constantly running, God becomes one more thing on our list, one more obligation to fulfill. I see it now in the way I pray or don't pray. I see it in how I rush through verses like I'm trying to get through a textbook. I see it in how Sunday mornings feel less like coming home and more like checking a box. Busyness has taught me to measure everything by productivity, including my walk with God. And I can't have a relationship with Him when I'm constantly measuring whether spending time with Him is 'worth it,' or 'efficient.'

The hardest part is that no one forces this on us. We do it to ourselves. We pack our schedules. We say yes to every opportunity. We pride ourselves on how much we can handle, how busy we are, how little sleep we need. And somewhere along the way, we lose the ability to just be still, to sit with God without an agenda, to spend time in His presence.

I'm not sure I have the answer yet. I'm still living in the busyness, still fighting the pull to fill every moment with productivity. But I'm starting to see that maybe the question isn't how to fit God into my busy life. Maybe the question is whether the life I'm living—this constant rushing, this endless striving—is the life God intended at all.

BRIAN

When I reflect on materialism's quieter dangers, I think of Brian. I met him in my earliest months here, an earnest, disciplined man of quiet integrity. He had felt the stress of poverty in his childhood home and had watched it affect the people he loved. He resolved, quietly and fiercely, to redirect his own story. Brian's drive for achievement wasn't fired by the sparkle of possessions or by a craving for status; it was a solid promise to himself and to those he left behind to give them the taste of security.

With a drive bordering on relentless, Brian pursued a career in finance and, season after season, climbed the corporate ladder. He was analytical, tireless, and masterful in his discipline. In a matter of years, he had secured wealth that previous generations of his family had only imagined. He could now buy the things that had once seemed impossible—penthouse apartments, expensive meals, flight after flight to islands he had never previously named. To onlookers, Brian's story was the opposite of failure.

Yet, as Brian's career climbed, his closeness to God that had once governed his life loosened its hold. He had once been the boy who sat in the same pew, who believed that prayer and communion could change the course of things. Slowly, his Saturdays and Sundays were taken over by conference calls and business breakfasts. The rhythm that had once ordered his weeks faded to a distant memory. The conversations about Scripture that had once filled late meals were crowded out by profit-and-loss statements, market analyses, and the race to spot the next winning investment.

Brian had not become a bad person; at heart, he remained the kind, generous man I had always admired. Yet the relentless pursuit of wealth had quietly, but clearly, changed his balance. The flow of his generosity had gradually narrowed to a trickle, absorbed now by the constant drive to grow his bank balance. The guy I once knew, eager to explore the quiet mysteries of faith and life, seemed to fade. Our conversations, once deep, now skimmed the surface. He talked, he gestured, he moved, but I sensed he was going through the motions, mechanically targeting the next goal without once pausing to be simply satisfied.

I can still recall the late-autumn evening when Brian parked his new car outside the café. Black paint gleaming, leather scent still fresh, it shone under the streetlights like a promise. Pride lit his face, and, almost against my will, a little excitement sparked in me too.

"Look what arrived," he said, the thrill of ownership spilling over.

I offered my congratulations, then, almost carefully, I asked, "Do you feel satisfied now?"

The silence that followed reminded me of the quietness of an empty church. He stood a moment, gaze drifting from the car to the pavement to the star-filled sky, his smile fading almost imperceptibly. Finally, he said, "Honestly? I thought I would. But I'm already picturing the next thing."

I had watched him chase things for years. The achievement he had pursued relentlessly, rarely with anything resembling rest, had become an unquenchable addiction. Every additional purchase brought with it a deepening unease. I could almost feel his emptiness. Beneath his confident gestures, he seemed to have lost his love of life.

What most surprised me was that Brian was following the herd. We are taught to believe that more—more money, more possessions, more status—will pay the debt of discontent. Yet, Brian was proving that it doesn't. In watching Brian, I discovered—perhaps too late—that my own desires were blurred. I kept judging Brian's climb, telling myself that his lifestyle was the problem. In truth, I was chasing the same prizes, convincing myself that the next achievement, the next promotion, the next reward, would finally unlock some need in my chest. I, too, had begun to give too much weight to things that had no real value. I no longer felt the warmth of friendship and the clarity of inward contentment. How many important conversations and unrepeatable moments had I passed over because I was running after a shadow that had quietly changed shape each time I reached for it?

Brian's story doesn't hide from hard emotions or difficult truths. Several years after reaching the financial goals he'd once dreamed about, and despite a comfortable bank account, he felt cold in the areas that once seemed inherent: his faith, his friendships, the sense of doing meaningful work. When he finally called, the conversation between us felt honest in a way it hadn't in far too long. He admitted, simply, that he had let the constant chase for profit drown out the deeper needs of his soul. That confession didn't land lightly; it became a turning point. Over the following months, Brian chose, day after day, to flip his priorities. He prioritized faith and community over ambition. Sunday attendance, once an afterthought, became a constant, and he joined a church outreach that teaches financial wisdom rooted in generosity. In the process, he didn't lose his skill with numbers but rediscovered its real purpose.

The change in Brian wasn't sudden; it unfolded quietly. He found his way back to his childhood church. He reconnected with family and friends. The road wasn't smooth; doubts came back as often as joys. Yet with each small, deliberate choice, he learned to shift his priorities off empty things and plant them on what the years had quietly shown to be solid—love, faith, and the warmth of shared moments. Watching him, I felt something stir in my own spirit. I had spent years polishing the outside and letting the deeper center gather dust. I was ready to get honest with my own path and to see, perhaps for the first time in too long, what I was really, finally seeking.

FULFILLMENT

Brian's journey continues to stand as a clear warning about the dangers of materialism. The pull of financial success can hook anyone, but its cost is often connection, purpose, and faith. Jesus warned about this exact trap: "No one can serve two masters, for either he will hate the one and love the other, or he will be devoted to the one and despise the other. You cannot serve God and money" (Matthew 6:24). Brian thought he was serving God while building wealth. He discovered, like the rich young ruler, that money had become his functional master. The difference is that Brian, unlike the young ruler, eventually turned back.

Brian's awakening—and the parallel one I began to experience—showed that real satisfaction doesn't come from the marketplace. What Brian discovered, and what I'm still learning, is that stewardship matters more than ownership. God doesn't call us to hoard wealth or chase after the next thing. He calls us to hold our resources with open hands, to use what we have to bless others, to recognize that everything we own is really His. Stewardship tells us to stop and ask: What is this for? Who does this serve? Am I managing God's resources well, or am I just feeding my own appetite?

Brian had to wrestle with those questions, and so do I. Every paycheck, every purchase, every financial decision is a chance to either worship at the altar of more or to practice the discipline of enough. It's a daily choice, and it's harder than it sounds because our culture screams at us that we need more, deserve more, should have more. Stewardship is not denying ourselves every good thing, but holding those good things loosely, not pretending money doesn't matter, but refusing to let it matter more than it should, and not avoiding success, but defining success by God's measure instead of the world's.

Brian's still on that journey. So am I. But watching him choose faith over finance and generosity over gain has shown me what's possible when we stop chasing what will never satisfy and start investing in what actually lasts. And busyness is not the answer.

INTEGRATING FAITH INTO DAILY LIFE, NOT ADDING MORE ACTIVITIES

Here's the trap most of us fall into: We think being a good Christian means doing more Christian things. Go to church on Sunday. Join a small group on Wednesday. Volunteer on Saturday. Add a Bible study. Squeeze in a prayer meeting. Before you know it, faith becomes another section on your calendar, another list of obligations competing for the same limited time you're already struggling to manage. But that's not what Jesus taught. He didn't say 'Come to me, all you who are weary and burdened, and I will give you more activities." He said, "Come to me, … and I will give you rest" (Matthew 11:28). These words should characterize our faith, not exhaust us. Rest. Not more busyness, even if that busyness is religious.

The problem is we've turned faith into something we do *instead of someone we're with*. We've made it about attending events instead of abiding in Christ. And when faith becomes just another item on our to-do list, it starts to feel like a burden instead of a joy. It becomes one more thing we're failing at when we can't keep up.

I see this all the time—people who are exhausted, burnt out, running on empty, and when you ask them about their faith, they feel guilty. Guilty that they're not reading their Bible enough. Guilty that they missed small group again. Guilty that they can't serve like they used to.[9] They love Jesus, but they're drowning, and the life raft they're being offered looks like more weight. This isn't what God wants. He doesn't want us to add Him to our

---

[9] Lifeway Research, "7 Reasons Churches Are Too Busy," *Lifeway Research*, November 23, 2016, https://research.lifeway.com/2016/11/23/7-reasons-churches-are-too-busy.

already overflowing schedule. He wants to be the center from which everything else flows. He wants to transform how we *live*.

So what does it look like to integrate faith into daily life instead of treating it as an add-on?

It starts with presence, not productivity.

Faith isn't measured by how many Christian activities you can cram into your week. It's measured by whether you're aware of God's presence in the ordinary moments. Brother Lawrence, a 17th-century monk, called this "practicing the presence of God." He spent his days washing dishes in a monastery kitchen, and he said he felt as close to God scrubbing pots as he did during formal prayer because he learned to be aware of God in everything he did. He didn't separate his "spiritual life" from his "regular life." It was all one life, lived in God's presence.

That's what we need to recover. Not more events, but more awareness. Not more programs, but more presence.

It means finding God in what you're already doing.

You're already working. You're already eating meals. You're already commuting, parenting, studying, resting. What if those ordinary moments became opportunities to connect with God?

Pray while you drive. Thank God for the food before you eat. Ask Him for wisdom before that difficult conversation. Worship while you fold laundry. Read a verse while you wait for your coffee to brew. These aren't adding activities to your schedule; they're inviting God into what's already there. The psalmist wrote, "When I consider your heavens, the work of your fingers, the moon and the stars, which you have set in place …" (Psalm 8:3). He saw creation and thought of God. That's integration. He didn't need to be in the temple to encounter God. He found Him in what was already in front of him.

It requires saying no to some things.

Here's the hard truth: If your life is so full that you have no space to breathe, you won't have room for God—not in any meaningful way. You can add more Christian activities, but you won't experience the life He's offering.

Integration requires subtraction, not addition. It means looking at your schedule and asking, "What can I let go of?" It means being willing to disappoint people, to turn down opportunities, to say, "I can't do that right now." This is countercultural. We live in a world that celebrates busyness, that equates value with productivity. But Jesus modeled something different. He withdrew to pray. He sent the crowds away. He took time to rest. And if the Son of God needed rhythms of rest and solitude, how much more do we?

It's about reordering, not just adding.

The problem isn't that we don't have time for God. The problem is that we've put other things first. We've organized our lives around work, around success, around keeping up appearances, around our kids' activities, and around our own comfort. And then we try to squeeze God into whatever's left. But Jesus said, "Seek first his kingdom and his righteousness, and all these things will be given to you as well" (Matthew 6:33). Jesus spent the whole Sermon on the Mount building to this point. 'Don't worry about what you'll eat or wear,' He said. 'Don't chase after what everyone else chases.' Instead, "Seek first the kingdom of God and his righteousness, and all these things will be added to you" (Matthew 6:32–34). First. Not 'fit it in where you can' or 'add it to your list.' First. That word reorders everything.

What would it look like to actually put God first? Not just say it, but live it? It might mean starting your day with Him before you check your phone. It might mean protecting Sunday as a day of rest instead of just another day to catch up. It might mean making financial decisions based on kingdom priorities instead of cultural expectations. It might mean choosing a less demanding job so you have more time for what matters.

These aren't easy choices, but they're the choices that lead to a life where faith is the foundation.

It's about abiding, not striving.

In John 15, Jesus uses the metaphor of a vine and branches. He says, "Abide in me, and I in you. As the branch cannot bear fruit by itself, unless it abides in the vine" (John 15:4). Notice what He doesn't say. He doesn't say 'Work harder for me.' He doesn't say 'Do more Christian activities.' He says, "Abide [remain] in me."

Abiding isn't about doing. It's about being. It's about staying connected to Jesus and letting His life flow through you. And when you're connected to Him, really connected, the fruit comes naturally. You don't have to manufacture it. You don't have to strive for it. It grows because you're rooted in the right place. This is the shift we need to make—from trying to be good Christians through effort and activity to simply staying close to Jesus and letting Him live through us to reordering our lives around Him.

It's not easier, necessarily, but it's sustainable. And it's what He's inviting us into.

WHAT CHURCH MEMBERS CAN DO: REORDER YOUR LIFE AROUND WHAT ACTUALLY MATTERS

Honestly, I'm still figuring this out. I'm still living in the pace of busyness. I'm still fighting the pull to fill every moment with productivity. But I've learned enough to know that the question isn't about how I fit God into my busy life. The question is whether the life I'm living is actually the life God wants for me.

Stop adding Christian activities and start subtracting everything else. You don't need more programs. You don't need more Bible studies or prayer meetings or volunteer opportunities. What you need is margin. Space. Breathing room. Look at your schedule honestly. What are you doing that isn't essential? What commitments can you let go of? What opportunities can you say no to? What can you stop doing so you have room to actually live?

This is hard because culture tells you that busyness equals importance and that productivity equals worth. But Jesus doesn't measure you that way. He doesn't measure you, period. He just loves you spending time with Him.

Find God in the ordinary moments you're already living. You don't need to add spiritual practices to your day. You need to invite God into what's already there. Pause and remember that God is present in everything.

Brother Lawrence lived in awareness of God's presence.

Be willing to disappoint people. Say no. Turn down opportunities. Admit you can't do something. Don't overcommit. This feels selfish in a culture that celebrates busyness. But it's not selfish. It's necessary. If you have no space to breathe, you won't have room for God—not in any meaningful way.

Reorder your life, don't just add to it. The problem isn't that you don't have time for God. The problem is that you've organized your life around other things—work, success, appearances, activities. And then you try to squeeze God into whatever's left.

What would it look like to actually put God first? Not just say it, but live it? You might face difficult choices, but they're the ones that create a life where faith is actually the foundation.

Practice presence, not productivity. Stop measuring your faith by how many Christian activities you can cram in. Measure it by whether you're aware of God's presence in ordinary moments. That's real faith. Not performance. Not achievement. Just presence.

Don't wait for your church to tell you how to pray or practice presence. Start with simple, doable practices you can actually sustain. Take three deep breaths and invite God into each moment. Set a phone alarm to pause and pray at certain times. Incorporate faith into family meals, commutes, and work breaks. Make it personal to your actual life, not an idealized version.

Think through your actual schedule, commitments, and energy levels. What does seeking God first look like in your specific situation? A single parent working two jobs has different rhythms than a retired couple. Figure out what works for you, not what works for someone else's life.

Honor the Sabbath for yourself. Rest isn't laziness, it's obedience. God commanded the Sabbath not because He's strict, but because He knows you need it. You need a day to forget productivity. Give yourself permission to rest. Remember that God delights in *you*, not just in what you accomplish.

If your church is making the Sabbath impossible—scheduling so many activities that you never get a day off—speak up. Talk to leadership. Advocate for change. Your rest matters.

Put God first in practice, not just theory. Evaluate your life honestly. What does it mean to seek God first in your finances? In your time? In your relationships? Make changes where needed. Look for stories of people who've reordered their lives or taken a pay cut for more family time, or who started giving sacrificially and saw God's provision. Let their courage give you courage.

Are you becoming more like Jesus, growing spiritually, and maintaining the relationships that matter most?

WHAT CHURCH LEADERS CAN DO: HELP YOUR CONGREGATION BREAK FREE FROM BUSYNESS

If you're honest with yourself, it's likely that your church is probably making busyness worse, not better. You're adding programs. You're filling schedules. You're celebrating how much your congregation is involved. And in doing so, you're teaching them that faith is about doing more Christian things, not about abiding in Christ. Your job is to help them break that cycle.

Stop adding programs and start cutting them. I know this feels counterintuitive. More programs mean more options, right? More engagement, more ministry, more impact? Wrong. More programs mean more busyness. More fragmentation. More exhaustion. More guilt when people can't keep up. Look at your church calendar honestly. Do you really need all of these programs? Are they serving people or exhausting them? Which programs are creating authentic community, and which are just filling slots?

Cut ruthlessly. Cut programs that aren't life-giving. Cut activities that are just habits. Cut things that keep people from resting. Then communicate why. Help your congregation understand that you're not cutting programs because faith doesn't matter. You're cutting them because you want faith to be something people actually experience, not just something they attend.

Teach integration, not addition. Stop inviting people to add more Christian activities to their already-full schedules. Teach them how to find God in the life they're already living. Preach about praying while they work, about seeing God in creation, about being aware of His presence throughout their day, about worshiping while they do ordinary tasks.

Help your congregation understand that faith isn't primarily about what they do on Sunday or Wednesday. It's about how they live every moment.

Make rest nonnegotiable. Protect Sunday. Don't fill it with meetings and programs and volunteer obligations. Make it a day of rest and worship, not a day of church busyness. Encourage your leaders to actually take time off. Model it yourself. Make it clear that rest isn't laziness. Rest is obedience. God commanded it. You need it. Help your congregation understand that if the Son of God needed rest and solitude, they do too.

Help people reorder their priorities, not just add to them. Help them examine what they've organized their lives around. What's actually first? What gets their time, energy, and resources?

Teach about seeking God's kingdom first, not as a nice idea, but as a radical reordering. What would it look like to actually live that? Help people ask hard questions, such as What financial decisions am I making? What job am I in? What commitments have I made? Are these choices aligned with putting God first, or are they pulling me away from Him?

Teach abiding, not striving. Stop talking about faith as something you achieve or accomplish. Stop measuring it by activity level or volunteer hours or program participation. Teach about abiding. About remaining connected to Jesus, about letting His life flow through them instead of constantly striving to do Christian things. Help your congregation understand that fruit, real spiritual fruit, comes from connection, not effort, and from presence, not productivity.

Preach honest sermons about your own struggle with busyness. Don't pretend you have this figured out. Talk about how you struggle with overcommitment. Share about the times you're so busy that your faith feels like a checkbox. Be honest about how hard it is to resist the pull of busyness.

When people see their leader wrestling with this, they get permission to wrestle too. They understand that it's not a personal failure; it's a cultural problem everyone is dealing with.

Create accountability for rest. Don't just recommend Sabbath, require it for yourself and your staff. Make rest nonnegotiable. Take it seriously. Protect it fiercely. Rest is how you stay connected to God. Rest is how you maintain perspective. Rest is how you love people well.

Measure success differently. Stop measuring by attendance and program participation. Start measuring by spiritual transformation, by depth of relationships, by whether people are actually experiencing God in their daily lives. Ask if people are overwhelmed or at peace, if they are experiencing God's presence or just checking boxes, if they are growing in their relationship with Christ or just busy with church activities.

THE HEART OF IT ALL

Busyness isn't just a time management problem. It's a spiritual problem. It's idolatry—worshiping at the altar of productivity instead of at the feet of Jesus.

Your job as a leader is to help your congregation break that cycle, not by adding more programs or more guilt, but by helping them see that the life God wants for them is simpler, slower, and more deeply rooted than the life culture is selling them.

That's how you help them experience real faith, not as performance, but as presence, not as achievement, but as abiding.

DISCUSSION QUESTIONS

1. Derrick describes how busyness became his "new religion" during boarding school. What has become your functional religion—the thing you actually organize your life around?

2. Brian's story shows how the pursuit of wealth can quietly displace faith. When have you experienced the emptiness of achieving something you thought would satisfy?

3. "We've turned faith into something we do instead of someone we're with." How does this show up in your life? What would change if you thought of faith as a relationship rather than an activity?

4. The chapter challenges readers to examine what they can subtract from their schedules, not just what to add. What would you need to say no to in order to create space for God?

5. "If your life is so full that you have no space to breathe, you won't have room for God." Be honest: Do you have space right now? What's preventing it?

6. Review your church's calendar. Is it helping people integrate faith into daily life, or is it just filling their schedules with more activities?

7. What would it look like for you to practice the presence of God in one ordinary activity this week?

CHAPTER 8

CREATING TRUE WELCOME

My switch to nondenominational Christianity wasn't just a change of churches; it was an entire restart of my faith. During my time in the Catholic Church, I felt like an outsider—going through the motions of rituals without understanding what I was doing. But as a Christian, I felt the chance for real participation, as I was given the opportunity to build a personal relationship with God. It was refreshing, as it let me truly explore my beliefs in a more freeing and deeper way.

I embraced nondenominational Christianity fully, and soon my favorite day of the week became Sunday. I looked forward to church for several reasons. First was the free breakfast they provided, especially meaningful to me as a child. It was a simple meal, but for kids, it felt like a feast. Breakfast at home, followed by a second breakfast at church! To me, that was the dream—double breakfasts. It was a huge reason to make sure I was at church every week.

The morning meals certainly played their part, but it was also the breakfast gatherings that brought schoolmates together. This made the experience even better for me. We would have fun together both before and after the service, laughing and running around. Coming for breakfast made it feel less like a religious duty and more like a fun community event. It was a way to build friendships and create a sense of belonging. It wasn't just attending the service; it was also the togetherness and the joy of connection that made the experience special. It was in this togetherness that memories were made.

What strikes me now, looking back, is how much that feeling of being welcome mattered. I didn't just show up; I wanted to be there. The difference between those two things is everything. In the Catholic church, I'd felt like I was watching from the outside, never quite sure if I belonged. But here, people knew my name. They smiled when they saw me. They saved me a seat at the breakfast table. They asked how my week went. Small things, maybe, but they added up to something powerful: the certainty that I was wanted.

Being welcome isn't just about someone saying hello at the door. It's about feeling like you fit, like there's a place carved out specifically for you. It's about walking in and knowing you'll find familiar faces, hearing your name called out, being included in the laughter and the stories. That's what those Sunday mornings gave me. They gave me a sense that I wasn't just allowed to be there; I was supposed to be there.

A WHOLE COMMUNITY

I remember the way the adults treated us kids. They didn't just tolerate us running around; they seemed genuinely happy we were there. They made space for our energy, our noise, our questions. They didn't make us feel like we were in the way or that church was something serious and somber that we were interrupting. They made it feel like our presence—loud, messy, full of life—was part of what made the community whole.

That feeling of welcome extended beyond the breakfast and the fun. It seeped into the service itself. When I had questions about what was being taught, people took time to explain. When I didn't understand a Bible passage, someone would sit with me and break it down in a way that made sense. I never felt stupid for not knowing. I never felt judged for being new to all of this. I felt welcomed into the process of learning, of growing, of figuring out what faith meant for me.

Having friendly, familiar faces around every Sunday made the experience comforting. It was more than the religious teaching; it was the strong bond that was built that I deeply valued. Sundays were filled with spiritual growth and friendship. These things, though simple, turned out to make a huge difference during those early years for me. The church was no longer just a building where services happened; it became the place that opened doors to my young world. It was a place I was able to grow and become strong in both my faith and my friendships.

Looking back, I realize that being welcomed was what allowed everything else to take root. The faith came because I felt safe to explore it. The friendships deepened because I felt like I belonged. The spiritual growth happened because I wasn't spending all my energy wondering if I was supposed to be there. I could just be present, open, and ready to receive what God wanted to teach me. That's the gift the church gave me—not just doctrine, not just community, but the foundational feeling that I was welcome.

Once you know you're welcome, everything else becomes possible.

INVISIBLE

Once I relocated to the US, I started searching for a church I could attend, and fortunately, I found one a stone's throw from my house. They greeted me at the door, and I was very pleased. However, no one else in the church spoke to me after the initial greeting. I tried going week after week, hoping things would change, but I started feeling out of place and tried to decide whether I should keep going at all. Was it my hair, my clothes, my outward appearance?

I'd walk in, sit down, sing the songs, hear the sermon, and walk out without a single meaningful interaction. No one asked my name. No one invited me to lunch. No one seemed to notice or care that I was there. I wasn't being judged for my appearance in an obvious way. No one told me to cut my hair or criticized how I dressed, but I was invisible, which is its own kind of judgment. The message was clear: *You're not interesting enough, familiar enough, or connected enough for us to bother with.* This experience helped me see and understand why my pastor back home stressed meeting and greeting newcomers. I did not know how lonely it could be walking into a church without someone going out of their way to say "welcome."

If I, as a believer, could feel that way, I kept wondering how a nonbeliever would experience the same situation—someone walking into a church for the first time, maybe at the lowest point in their life, looking for hope or connection or just a place to belong. They're already nervous, already feeling like they don't fit. And then we confirm their worst fears by ignoring them completely or, worse, by making them feel judged for not looking like us. This isn't just unfriendly. It's antithetical to the gospel. Jesus had a habit of seeing the invisible. He noticed Zacchaeus up in a tree when everyone else ignored him. He stopped for the woman with chronic bleeding when everyone else pushed past her. He called out the widow putting in her two coins when everyone else watched the wealthy.

Seeing people—truly seeing them—is how Jesus loved. It's how He still loves. And it's how we're meant to love.

WELCOME

A church should embrace and cultivate a climate that fosters acceptance and encourages new and prospective attendees to return. This act, small as it may be, is suggestive of the love of Jesus, a love that is limitless, welcoming, and makes the person feel important and appreciated. Welcoming everyone should not be an event but a process that does not have an end, so bonds are forged and people are integrated into a community they can call a family.

Creating this kind of environment isn't complicated, but it does require intentionality. It requires building cultures where welcome isn't just a greeting at the door but a posture that permeates everything we do.

WHAT CHURCH MEMBERS CAN DO: BECOME A CONNECTOR

Welcome isn't something only designated greeters should do. Every person in your church has the power to make someone feel like they belong. Here's how:

Adopt a newcomer. Pick one new person each month and intentionally invest in knowing them. Not in a creepy way, just genuine interest. Text them once during the week. Invite them to do something ordinary together: grab coffee, go for a walk, attend a weekday event. Be the person who remembers they exist outside of Sunday morning.

Build your own welcome ecosystem around your circle. You don't need church leadership permission to create belonging. If you're in a small group or ministry team, make it your culture to notice who's new, follow up when someone stops coming, and actively include the quiet person who's on the edge. One welcoming circle can change someone's entire church experience.

Track what actually keeps people coming back. Pay attention: Is it the sermon? The music? The people? The practical details like childcare or accessible parking? Ask a new person directly: "What made you come back? What almost kept you away?" Their answers tell you what matters. Share those insights with your small group or leadership.

Create natural gathering spaces. Host things at your home. Organize a church game night. Start a coffee run before service. Create opportunities for people to connect in low-pressure environments where they can be themselves. Sometimes people connect over shared interests or activities faster than they do in formal church settings.

Know what helps your church fail at welcome. Be honest about your church's blind spots. Do you welcome people with disabilities? Are there unspoken dress codes? Is your church primarily one ethnicity or socioeconomic background? Do you lose people after the first visit? Name these things. Talk about them. You can't fix what you won't acknowledge.

WHAT CHURCH LEADERS CAN DO: ENGINEER WELCOME INTO YOUR DNA

As a leader, you're not just making people feel welcome; you're also building systems that make it nearly impossible for someone to slip through the cracks. Here's what that looks like:

Map the entire newcomer journey and remove friction. From the moment someone googles your church to the moment they leave their first Sunday, document every step. What's on your website? How easy is it to find parking? Where do they check in? How do they know where to go? Walk through this journey yourself. Better yet, have someone new walk through it and give you feedback. Each friction point is a reason someone might not come back.

Create a digital system that tracks actual welcome metrics. Most churches track attendance. You should track:

- How many first-time visitors became second-time visitors?
- Of those, how many became regular attenders?
- Of the regular attenders, how many joined a small group or ministry?
- Where do people drop off?

This data tells you exactly where your welcome breaks down.

Build a welcome pathway with clear handoffs. First visit → greeter makes note → follow-up team contacts them within 48 hours → integration team invites them to one small group or meal within two weeks → assignment to a mentor or small group leader → regular check-ins at one month, three months, six months. Each step has a person responsible. With no handoff, someone falls through the cracks.

Stop treating the lobby as a hallway and start treating it as a sanctuary. What happens between when service ends and when people leave? Is that where welcome happens? Or are people rushing to the next event? Consider keeping people in the lobby for 15–20 minutes after service with refreshments and an informal gathering space. Train your team to use that time intentionally. Some of your best connections will happen there.

Audit your communications for accessibility. Can someone navigate your church website without having grown up in church? Do your sermon slides have captions for deaf attendees? Are your printed materials available in languages spoken in your community? Do you describe important visual elements for blind attendees? Accessibility isn't an add-on; it's a foundational welcome.

Create a "first-time visitor experience" that's different from regular attendance. Consider a special welcome packet, a brief orientation before service, or a post-service conversation with a pastor or leader. Make first-timers feel like their visit matters enough to be noticed. Then track whether they return.

Measure the diversity of your welcome team. Who greets people? Who follows up? Who leads small groups? If your welcome infrastructure is staffed by the same type of person (same age, background, personality type, socioeconomic status), you're going to miss people who don't connect with that demographic. Diversify your teams intentionally.

Build welcome into staff evaluations and compensation. If you have paid staff, their performance review should include how many newcomers they've personally connected with and how many of those newcomers are still attending three months later. Make it part of everyone's job description, not just the welcome team's.

Create a "welcome crisis response" protocol. If a first-time visitor doesn't return after three visits, assign someone to personally reach out. Call them. Text them. Find out what happened. Was it something about the church? A personal circumstance? A barrier you didn't know existed? You won't fix every situation, but you might fix most of them, and you'll learn invaluable information about what's actually happening.

THE HEART OF IT ALL

Welcome isn't complicated. It's just seeing people and making them feel wanted. It's noticing who's alone and doing something about it. It's building systems that make belonging automatic instead of optional.

That's how you create the environment where faith can take root, not through perfect doctrine or impressive programs but through genuine community where people know they're seen, they're wanted, and they belong.

That's the gift every church should give.

DISCUSSION QUESTIONS

1. What's one specific barrier that makes your church harder to access than it needs to be? (It might be physical, cultural, technological, or social.) What's one step you could take to remove it?

2. Derrick felt invisible in one church but deeply wanted in another. What's the difference in how the two churches handled newcomers? What's the smallest thing that made the biggest difference?

3. If you looked at your church's "newcomer dropout curve" of how many people visit once but never return, what would it look like? What do you think happens between their first and second visit, or their decision not to come back?

4. Who in your church or leadership team should be responsible for ensuring newcomers are integrated, not just greeted? Do they currently have the time, authority, and resources to actually do this work?

5. Imagine you're a single parent with tattoos, limited income, and no church background, visiting your church for the first time. Walk through that person's experience from parking to leaving. Where would they feel welcome? Where might they feel like they don't belong?

6. "Welcome is something you have to intentionally build into your culture and your systems." What systems does your church currently have around welcome? Where are the gaps?

7. If you could only implement one structural change to improve welcome in your church, what would have the biggest impact? What would it take to make that happen?

CONCLUSION

FROM RITUAL TO RELATIONSHIP

I began this journey in the front pew of a Catholic church, a young boy performing rituals I didn't understand, feeling the weight of adult eyes on my back, squirming under expectations I couldn't meet. Church felt like crossing into another realm—beautiful, yes, with its architecture and stained glass—but distant. Sacred, but not personal. I went through the motions, checked the boxes, and wished I could stay home. I didn't know then that faith could be anything else.

My story—from that lonely front pew to a nondenominational Christian church where double breakfasts and genuine friendship made Sunday the best day of the week, from Uganda to the United States, from confused child to questioning adult—is a story of transformation. Not from bad to good, or wrong to right, but from ritual to relationship, from performing faith to experiencing it, and from trying to earn God's approval to discovering I was already loved unconditionally.

That transformation didn't happen because I finally got everything right. It happened because I encountered imperfect, messy, but genuine communities where people made space for me, my questions, and my doubts. Here, my appearance didn't determine my worth. I could show up as I was and found that I was enough.

I've written about the barriers I've encountered and witnessed: judgment based on appearance, finances, and past mistakes. Intellectual doubts that go unaddressed. Cultural expectations that force impossible choices. Leadership failures that shatter trust. Political divisions that tear families apart. Digital feeds that warp perceptions. Busyness that crowds out God. Materialism that promises satisfaction but delivers emptiness. And beneath all of it, the simple, devastating experience of walking into a room and realizing no one sees you, no one wants you, no one cares if you stay or go.

These barriers are real. They're high. They're doing damage every single day. But they're not insurmountable. Bridges can be built. Doors can be opened. People can be welcomed home.

That's what I believe. That's what I've seen. That's what I'm asking you—whether you're part of a church or searching for one, whether you're leading or following, whether you're confident in your faith or barely hanging on—to believe too.

But this isn't just about individual hurt or personal welcome. When we build barriers, the cost goes far beyond the people we exclude. It damages the church itself. It diminishes the gospel.

THE COST WE'RE NOT TALKING ABOUT

Think about the people your church is driving away right now. People who look different, who need answers, who think differently. Future leaders, mentors, thinkers, teachers who might have spent their lives serving God but instead opted out entirely, not because they rejected Jesus, but because they rejected us.

When churches become more exclusive, the gospel doesn't just reach fewer people; it actually becomes smaller. It stops being the radical, expansive, "whosoever will" message of grace and transforms into something domesticated, something manageable, something that fits neatly into our cultural preferences. We're saying the gospel is for certain kinds of people in certain kinds of circumstances who believe in certain kinds of ways. That's not the gospel. That's a club membership program.

The world doesn't need another exclusive club. It has plenty of those already. What the world desperately needs is one place where the barriers come down, where people don't have to perform or conform or clean up before they're welcomed. That place is supposed to be the church.

Our credibility is built on one thing: Do we actually live what we teach? Right now, the answer is increasingly no. And people see it. We're making it harder for people to believe.

TO THE CHURCH: ARE YOU BUILDING BRIDGES OR BARRIERS?

If you're reading this as a church leader, a member, or someone who's been part of a Christian community for years, I want to ask you the hardest question in this book:

Are you building bridges or barriers?

I don't ask this to accuse or condemn. I ask because I've been on both sides. I've been the one who felt judged for my Afro, who couldn't get my tattooed friend to visit because I knew how he'd be received, who sat invisible in a church week after week while everyone else enjoyed their established friendships. But I've also been the insider, comfortable in my own community, unaware of how my comfort was someone else's exclusion. I didn't see the barriers I was creating because they felt normal to me. They were just "how we do things."

That's the thing about barriers—you don't notice them until you're on the outside trying to get in.

I know most of you aren't trying to hurt anyone. You genuinely believe you're welcoming. You smile at the door. You shake hands. You say, "Glad you're here." Your intentions are good. But good intentions don't protect people from feeling judged. When the result is that people leave feeling unwanted, unseen, or judged unworthy of belonging, it doesn't matter much whether we meant it that way.

We don't mean to judge; we're just maintaining standards we think are important. We don't mean to exclude; we're just comfortable with people like us. We don't mean to drive people away; we're just doing church the way we've always done it. But the result is the same. The barriers stay up, and people keep walking away. So we need to examine everything and see clearly.

Look at your assumptions about what a Christian should look like, how they should dress, what they should believe about politics, how much they should give, what their past should look like, and what questions they're allowed to ask. Ask yourself honestly: Are these biblical requirements or cultural preferences? Are we guarding the gospel or guarding our comfort?

Look at your leadership. Who has power? Who has a voice? Who's visible? If everyone looks the same, thinks the same, votes the same, and reflects your own background and perspective, you might not be reflecting the kingdom of God. You might be reflecting your own tribe. And everyone who doesn't fit that tribe is getting a message, whether you intend it or not, that they don't belong here.

Look at how you welcome newcomers. Look at your programming. Look at your online presence. What message are you sending? I think about what Eugene Peterson called a tourist life—all surfaces, no depth. That's what social media pushes us toward. But Jesus reserved His harshest critique for surface religion. If we're only showing polished versions of faith online, people can tell the difference between a real community and a curated image. And they're voting with their feet.

This examination will be uncomfortable. You'll discover things you don't want to see. You'll realize you've hurt people without meaning to. You'll have to choose between making changes and losing people who are comfortable with things as they are. That's genuinely hard. I'm not minimizing that. But I've seen that when churches choose to do this hard work, something beautiful happens. Barriers come down. Communities become genuine. Faith becomes real. People start to experience the kingdom of God.

I know it's hard. I know it's costly. I know it requires humility to admit we've been getting it wrong, courage to make changes, and perseverance to keep going when it gets messy. I also know that you're probably doing better than you think. Most of you care deeply about people. Most of you are trying. Most of you would be heartbroken to know you'd hurt someone with your barriers.

But I also know that trying isn't enough. Love has to be more than intention. Love has to be visible, tangible, actual. When we build barriers instead of bridges, we're not protecting the gospel; we're protecting ourselves. We're creating safe spaces for people like us, comfortable communities where we don't have to be challenged or changed. But safety isn't what the gospel offers. Challenge is. Transformation is.

Jesus promised us tribulation. He promised us that following Him would cost us everything. But He also promised us that in the midst of that cost, we'd find abundance, community, purpose, and love. What we've done instead is create the illusion of safety by surrounding ourselves only with people who confirm what we already believe. We've mistaken comfort for faith. We've confused community with conformity.

But I've seen glimpses of what the church could be. I've seen churches where a former addict stands next to a banker and they embrace like brothers. Where a Republican and a Democrat serve on the same board and actually listen to each other. Where someone from a completely different faith tradition walked in carrying skepticism and walked out carrying hope. Where a young person with the "wrong" appearance and uncomfortable questions was welcomed. In those moments, I felt what the kingdom of God should feel like—real.

That's the power of the church when we embody the gospel, but that power is available to us only if we're willing to pay the cost of building bridges instead of maintaining barriers.

The world is watching. Your neighbors are watching. The seekers, the doubters, the wounded, the marginalized are all watching to see if we mean what we say about love and grace and welcome. They're watching because they want to believe. They want to find a place where they belong. They want to encounter Jesus.

Build bridges. Tear down barriers. Open doors. Make space. See people. Welcome strangers. Honor questions. Embrace complexity. Lead with love. Be the church that makes people say, "See how they love one another," instead of "If Christians can't get along, why would I join them?"

I'm not asking for perfection. I'm asking for faithfulness. I'm asking for the willingness to keep examining, keep learning, keep repenting, keep reaching. I'm asking for the humility to admit when you've created barriers and the courage to take them down.

That's my challenge to you. That's my prayer for you.

FROM RITUAL TO RELATIONSHIP

TO THE SEEKER: GOD'S KINGDOM IS FOR YOU

If you're reading this as someone on the outside—someone who's been hurt by the church, turned away, judged, excluded, or simply ignored—I want you to hear this clearly:

God's kingdom is for you.

Not the version of you that churches sometimes demand, cleaned up, figured out, perfectly conforming to cultural expectations. The actual you. The you with questions and doubts. The you with tattoos or an unconventional hairstyle. The you who's made mistakes and carries regrets. The you who doesn't have it all together. The you who's wondering if there's really room for someone like you in this faith.

You. Exactly as you are. Right now.

I know that might be hard to believe. I know you've probably encountered Christians who made you feel like you had to change before God would accept you. I know you've seen the hypocrisy, the judgment, the division. I know you've watched the scandals and the failures and wondered why anyone would want to be part of this mess. I know because I've been there too. I've stood on both sides of this divide. I've felt the sting of religious judgment. I've watched friends walk away from faith because the church made them feel unwanted. I've questioned whether it was all worth it. But here's what I've discovered: The church's failure to welcome you doesn't change God's heart toward you.

Jesus looked at a Samaritan woman with a complicated past and offered her living water. He welcomed tax collectors and prostitutes to His table. He touched lepers. He defended an adulterous woman from a stone-throwing crowd. He called fishermen and zealots and doubters to follow Him. He didn't wait for them to clean up their lives first. He invited them as they were and let transformation happen along the way, in community, through relationship.

That's the Jesus I follow. That's the Jesus I'm inviting you to encounter, not through the lens of broken churches or failed leaders, but directly, personally, honestly.

You don't have to have all the answers. You don't have to resolve all your doubts. You don't have to understand everything about theology or the Bible or how faith works. You don't have to change your appearance or abandon your questions or pretend you're someone you're not. You just have to be willing to take one step forward, to consider the possibility that there's more to this faith than what you've seen, to give Jesus a chance, even if you're not sure about His followers.

I'm not promising you'll find a perfect church. You won't. Churches are full of unhealed people who are still learning, still growing, still messing up and needing grace. But I am promising that if you seek God with an open heart, He will meet you. Not someday when you're ready. Not after you've figured everything out but right now, in the middle of your mess, with all your questions and doubts and fears.

He's already there, actually. He's been there all along, waiting for you, wanting to spend time with you, not because you've earned it or deserve it, but because that's who He is. That's what grace means.

So if you're reading this and you're wondering if there's room for you, there is. If you're carrying wounds from church experiences, He sees them and He cares. If you're tired of religion but still curious about relationship, that curiosity is an invitation. If you're skeptical but something in you hopes it might be true, that hope is enough to start with.

Find a community that reflects Jesus. They exist. They're rare, maybe, but they're out there—churches where questions are welcome, where doubts are safe, where people are valued for who they are, not who they might become. Keep looking. And in the meantime, start your own conversation with God. Read the Gospels—Matthew, Mark, Luke, John—and see Jesus for yourself, not filtered through anyone else's interpretation. Talk to Him honestly about your doubts, your anger, your questions. He can handle it. He's not fragile.

Listen for His voice in the quiet moments. Look for His presence in unexpected places. Pay attention to the pull you feel toward something more, something real, something that might actually satisfy the hunger that nothing else has filled.

That pull? That's Him. That's the Spirit drawing you home. And home is where you belong.

DISCUSSION QUESTIONS

For Individual Reflection

1. When you think about your own church experience, did you feel like Derrick in the Catholic church (performing, unsure if you belonged) or like him in the nondenominational Christian church (welcomed, known, eager to return)? What made the difference?

2. Derrick describes feeling invisible despite attending week after week. Have you ever felt invisible in a space where you thought you'd find community? What would have helped?

3. What does "being welcomed" actually mean to you, not in theory, but in your lived experience?

4. The author distinguishes between "showing up" and "wanting to be there." Which describes your current relationship with your church community?

5. Who in your life has made you feel genuinely wanted? What specifically did they do?

6. Looking at your own church or community, who might be feeling invisible right now? What small action could you take this week to help them feel seen?

For Group Conversation

1. Share about a time you felt genuinely welcomed into a community. What specifically happened?
2. Derrick talks about the difference between being "tolerated" and being "wanted." Has your church ever communicated, intentionally or not, that certain people are tolerated rather than wanted?
3. The author describes how his integration changed when he saw a leader who looked like him. What role does representation play in helping people feel welcome?
4. Derrick was told he should keep coming back, but his experience made him want to leave. How often do we tell people they're welcome while our systems communicate the opposite?
5. If you're a leader or longtime member: How might your church feel to a complete stranger walking in for the first time?
6. The conclusion emphasizes that transformation happened through genuine community, not because Derrick "got everything right." What does that suggest churches should actually focus on?

For Leadership Teams

1. How intentional are we about welcome? Is it something that happens naturally, or do we have systems in place to make it inevitable?
2. When we measure success, do we track integration of newcomers or just attendance?
3. Are there people currently attending our church who might feel invisible? How would we know?
4. Derrick's church created space for him beyond Sunday service (breakfast gatherings, friendships, adults who knew him). What informal spaces and relationships does our church create?
5. The author describes feeling unwelcome despite being a believer. How much harder must it be for someone exploring faith for the first time? What barriers might we be creating?
6. If we had to honestly assess whether our church reflects "radical welcome" or something more exclusive, what would we say? Where are we falling short?

For Seekers

1. Has your experience with church matched Derrick's description of being invisible? What would be different for you to feel like you belonged?
2. The author describes finding a community where he felt safe to explore faith. What kind of environment would make you feel safe?
3. What questions or doubts are you carrying that you think would make you unwelcome in a church?
4. If you decided to explore Christianity, what would you need from a community? What would keep you coming back?

A FINAL NOTE

I don't know what brought you to this book. Maybe you're sitting in that lonely front pew like I was. Maybe you're the outsider wondering if there's room for you. Maybe you're the insider realizing for the first time that you've been creating the barriers. Whoever you are, this is my invitation to you: Don't give up on God or on the church.

My teammate never came back to church. I think about that sometimes, not with guilt, but with determination, because I know what he's missing isn't perfection. It's belonging. And belonging is something we can actually build, one welcome at a time. That's where it starts. That's where it always starts.

The barriers are real. The hurt is real. The failures of the church are real. But so is the possibility of something different. I've seen it. I've lived it. And I believe you can too.

The church Jesus envisioned isn't waiting for perfect people. It's waiting for brave ones. Brave enough to see differently. Brave enough to welcome differently. Brave enough to believe that change is possible. The question now is: what will you do with what you've read? Who will you see? What barrier will you tear down?

Are you ready?

ABOUT THE AUTHOR

Derrick Kitayiga is an emerging cybersecurity expert currently pursuing a bachelor of science in cybersecurity at California State University, San Marcos. As a California Department of Public Health information technology associate, he helps protect and enhance critical systems and contributes to efforts that serve and safeguard communities across California.

A natural storyteller, Derrick weaves together experiences, lessons, and reflections from both technology and the human journey, offering a perspective shaped by observation, empathy, and lived experience. Guided by his Christian faith, he approaches life and work with integrity and a deep concern for how people feel welcomed, valued, and connected. His own experiences within faith communities give him a unique understanding of what draws people in and what unintentionally pushes them away.

Whether writing about belonging, welcome, or the barriers that keep people from church, Derrick speaks with compassion and clarity, inviting leaders and members alike to see their communities through fresh eyes. He also plays soccer to cultivate discipline, resilience, and teamwork—qualities he consistently demonstrates.

Committed to pursuing the "good side" of cybersecurity and the good of the church, Derrick brings a thoughtful, faith-centered lens to the challenges of connection and retention, helping churches create environments where people can grow and remain rooted.

Online Presence:

Email: Kitayigaderrick9@icloud.com
Instagram: DerrickUganda
Facebook: Kitayiga Derrick M.

OTHER BOOKS BY DERRICK KITAYIGA

Derrick Kitayiga woke up one morning from what he now sees as a God-sent dream. But a dream of moving from Kampala, Uganda, to the West is one thing; seeing it come to pass is quite another.

In *I Dreamed of Skyscrapers,* Kitayiga paints a vivid picture of the transformative and hope-filled power of faith. The author navigates through many obstacles—betrayal, grief, theft of his savings, and lack of support he could count on, and yet he persevered. Set against the backdrop of two drastically different worlds, this compelling narrative of perseverance is about holding onto dreams, and finding the strength to keep pushing forward.

If you are struggling to hold steadfast to your faith, let Derrick Kitayiga's uplifting story serve as an inspirational beacon to guide you to the fulfillment of your own dreams.

www.ingramcontent.com/pod-product-compliance
Lightning Source LLC
Chambersburg PA
CBHW070629030426
42337CB00020B/3964